The Kingdom of God Suffers Violence!

The Kingdom of God Suffers Violence!

FAITHFUL BELIEVERS PRESS THROUGH THE NARROW GATE AND THE DIFFICULT WAY TO GOD'S KINGDOM!

John Elliott Williams

"And from the days of John the Baptist until now the kingdom of heaven suffers violence, and the violent *take it by force*" Matthew 11:12(NKJV).

The Kingdom of God Suffers Violence!
By John Elliott Williams
Printed in the United States of America

ISBN-13: 9781519438478
ISBN-10: 1519438478
Library of Congress Control Number: 2015919523
CreateSpace Independent Publishing Platform
North Charleston, South Carolina

For information regarding this book and the author, contact John Elliott Williams, elliottlabor1@bellsouth.net or 678-561-8978

The way to Life is Difficult!

Matthew 7:13-14 (NKJV) - "Enter by the narrow gate; for wide is the gate and broad is the way that leads to destruction, and there are many who go in by it. Because narrow is the gate and _difficult_ is the way which leads to life, and _there are few who find it._"

In Memory Of Diane!

IN OCTOBER OF 2013, MY older sister, Diane Williams Ward passed away from this world. Her assignment and time had been completed. I believe with all my heart that Diane is among those *dead in Christ* waiting for the resurrection with all the other saints. Diane didn't preach or teach God's Word, but she lived a life of a faithful believer, sang in a gospel choir and demonstrated the characteristics of a born-again believer who knew to bear the fruits of the Holy Spirit! "But the fruit of the Spirit is love, joy, peace, longsuffering, kindness, goodness, faithfulness, gentleness, and self-control. Against such there is no law" Galatians 5:22-23 (NKJV). In her dying days, Diane's peace and longsuffering revealed the presence of the Lord by her side. God's Spirit really does give <u>comfort</u> in times of affliction!

Diane was a quiet- spirited person who chose not to fight or battle in words, but to live and let live. She loved the Lord with all her heart while being content with the things God provided for her and her son, Gregory. Diane encountered a lot of illnesses in her later years, yet she remained *faithful* to God and was a pleasant light of joy for others to see. I miss my sister, but I also know that God gives us only a short time on earth to learn, mature and demonstrate the character of Jesus Christ. This is what the Gospel is all about! I believe Diane met the goals of the Father and one day we will be reunited together again as sons and daughters of God!

See you later Diane!

Introduction

PERHAPS, ONE OF THE MOST difficult changes a believer can make in life is their theology! For years the church has promoted God's blessings, human development, prosperity, and all the things the world enjoys. However, this form of teaching draws a thin line between God's intended sacrificial living versus the desires and the lusts of the flesh as sinful natured creatures! Promoting things of the flesh causes humans to _desire_ the things of the world more than seeking God's Kingdom and the things God provides. The things God provide are enough.. God's Spirit directs our lives through the gifts and talents Jesus Christ gives us to live on this earth. Therefore, as Christian believers, we do not have to submit ourselves to the world's lust, greed, control, selfishness and other acts that separate us from God. Jesus offers His kingdom! "But seek first the kingdom of God and His righteousness, and all these things shall be added to you" Matthew 6:33 (NKJV). To keep us from lusting for more, one must hear from God's Spirit when moving into one's calling which might be a rich entrepreneur, an actor, a professional sport's hero or one who leads a nation. Believers must make sure these aspirations come from God so we will not prostitute the gifts. God gives us the gifts and talents for the benefit of His Kingdom and to transform believers into the _salt_ and _light_ of the earth. In the Lord's teaching, _salt_ symbolizes spiritual health and vigor, which is essential to Christian virtue and counteractive of the world's corruption. Metaphorically, the _light_ represents their character and spiritual condition.

Believers Are Salt and Light

"You are the salt of the earth; but if the salt loses its flavor, how shall it be sea-soned? It is then good for nothing but to be thrown out and trampled underfoot by men. "You are the light of the world. A city that is set on a hill cannot be hid-den. Nor do they light a lamp and put it under a basket, but on a lampstand, and it gives light to all who are in the house" Matthew 5:13-15 (NKJV)

The *light* is of God's truth and its knowledge together with the spiritual purity that which is exposed to the view of all. *Light* is also a spiritual mind with the power to understand moral and spiritual truth. Therefore, if our salt loses its flavor and our light is hidden under a basket, believers become "good for nothing" and *I will leave it at that!*

Unfortunately, many of God's servants have moved away from the things which God's Word clearly reveals in our redemption process and the pathway to getting there! Preaching and teaching the lighter side of the Gospel, which is God's blessings and His provisions on earth, rather than revealing how believers become living sacrifices, holy and acceptable to God can lead one to Satan's influence. Furthermore, preaching these messages makes the things of this world of more importance! They give credence to bigger homes and cars, entertainment, life styles of the rich and famous, body development and outward beauty as more valuable than becoming an over-comer who lives sacrificially. You are an over-comer when you stand on God's Word in faith, obedience and dependence on the Lord. This is where the Holy Spirit can deliver believers from the lusts of their flesh and the corruption of this world. When the believers live according to God's Spirit in holy sacrifice, they are acceptable to God.

A Living Sacrifice to God

"I beseech you therefore, brethren, by the mercies of God, that you present your bodies a living sacrifice, holy, acceptable to God, which is your reasonable service. And do not be conformed to this world, but be transformed by the renewing of your mind, that you may prove what is that good and acceptable and perfect will of God" Romans 12:1-2 (NKJV).

Satan would love for all Christians to be earthly minded and seeking the riches of this world instead of preparing themselves as children of God for our new beginning. We only have a few years on this earth, some less than others, to prove ourselves worthy to become sons and daughters of God. This world is not our home; *it is a stop-over* for those who trust in the Lord and are faithful and obedient to God's Word. I am not sure how many Christians look at this world that way? I am sorry if they do not because no one will inherit God's Kingdom and see the new heaven and earth but *obedient believers!* You may hear a lot of sermons to contradict this truth, but read Jesus' parable of the ten virgin with spiritual understanding and you will clearly see who attends the wedding supper of the Lamb.

There are two Scriptures every Christian should be mindful of and know their spiritual meaning and interpretation. The first Scripture was spoken by God to Adam. "Then to Adam He said, "Because you have heeded the voice of your wife, and have eaten from the tree of which I commanded you, saying, 'You shall not eat of it': "Cursed is the ground *for your sake* in toil you shall eat of it all the days of your life. Both thorns and thistles it shall bring forth for you" Genesis 3:17-18 (NKJV). When God spoke the words of the Scripture to Adam, He was advising Him and all creation that the earth was cursed and that it would bring toil, sorrows, pain, labor and hardship. The thorns and thistles which God spoke of produce a physical, painful and humiliating life. These hardships and sorrows are also the effects of divinely permitted satanic antagonism. Thorns are a thorny or prickly plant. They are sharp and cause pain, irritation, discomfort and sometimes cause distress or irritation. They represent an adverse life for all who live on the earth.

Theoretically, God was saying to Adam, "This is the life that you and future generations will live on the earth. You will live with trials, tests, sorrows, tribulations, afflictions, chastisements, sufferings and the like, all the days of your life *for your sake and your seed!* This means that humanity must *press through* these adversities in order to enter God's Kingdom. Simply speaking, we must endure! Jesus acknowledged that the road to *life* is narrow and difficult. To strengthen the souls of the disciples, exhorting them to continue in the faith, the Apostle Paul added, "We must through many tribulations enter the kingdom of God" Acts 14:22 (NKJV). As believers, we prove our faithfulness to God when we endure the hardships and afflictions of this world and still maintain our belief in Jesus Christ. Most people, even Christians, do not care to talk about human suffering as part of God's plan on the earth, yet it is. You will learn from this book that Christians must press through the many obstacles we face to serve in God's Kingdom as victims of sacrificial living. Jesus spoke these words to His disciples, "But he who endures to the end shall be saved" Matthew 24:13 (NKJV).

This is why we must seek God's Kingdom, pursue and endure to the end. To seek is to aim or strive after. It is crave or demand something from someone. To pursue is to seek eagerly, earnestly and endeavor to acquire. They all have similar characteristics. A believer must seek God's Kingdom by craving, pursuing, demanding, and striving after it. It is done within one's own heart, mind and soul by thinking, praying, studying God's Word, meditating, reasoning, inquiring and asking God for spiritual insight and revelation. Mostly, it is changing your life according to the leading and guiding of God's Spirit. The difficult way to life in God's Kingdom means that an individual must exhaust energy and effort to enter it. Nothing comes easy! You must take the Kingdom by force of heart, mind and soul.

Disobedience in the Garden of Eden meant that man had to be redeemed back to God in order to become worthy sons and daughters. This redemption process requires believers to be _Spirit-filled_ again as they were before the fall! Humans were created in God's image and likeness which is being Spirit-filled. "Then God said, "Let Us make man in Our image, according to Our likeness; let them have dominion over the fish of the sea, over the birds of the air, and over the cattle, over all the earth and over every creeping thing that creeps on the earth." So God created man in His own image; in the image of God He created him; male and female He created them" Genesis 1:26-27 (NKJV). Many of today's Christians do not know or understand that God returned His Spirit to humans as the Holy Spirit...a Comforter, guide and the source of power to become His children. Many Christians continue to live as natural beings (sinful flesh creatures) that live according to their carnal minds. *Only* Spirit-filled believers can become sons and daughters of God. "Therefore, brethren, we are debtors—not to the flesh, to live according to the flesh. For if you live according to the flesh you will die; but if by the Spirit you put to death the deeds of the body, you will live. For as many as are led by the Spirit of God, these are sons of God" Romans 8:12-14 (NKJV).

Even though God's people must endure many trials, for a little while [their time on earth], these trials will show whether their faith is *genuine*. Therefore, when a believer's faith remains strong through many trials, that strength will bring them much praise, glory and honor on the day Jesus Christ is revealed to the world. For the way to *life* in God's Kingdom is rendered as *narrowed* by Divine conditions which makes it impossible for anyone to enter, who thinks entrance to depends upon self-merit. Neither is it for *those* who are still inclined towards sin or the desire to continue in evil. As I have stated before, it just will not happen! As a people, the earth may be cursed and the way to life may be difficult, but God gave us Jesus Christ to cover our sins and His Spirit to direct our lives so that we may live in power..

The very day we believed in Jesus as Lord and Savior of our life, God sealed us with His Spirit until the day of Redemption. "In Him you also trusted, after you heard the word of truth, the gospel of your salvation; in whom also, having believed, you were sealed with the Holy Spirit of promise, who is the guarantee of our inheritance until the redemption of the purchased possession, to the praise of His glory" Ephesians 1:13-14 (NKJV). Believing in Jesus and receiving God's Spirit means we no longer belong to ourselves because we have become God's property. We were bought with a price. However, many Christians do not know they are sealed by God's Spirit. Being *sealed* means ownership and security, together with destination as servants. Because many do not know, they carelessly grieve and/or quench the fiery action of the Holy Spirit. This causes a multitude of spiritual issues for the believer which is further explained later in this book.

A quenched or extinguished Spirit will not lead and guide the flesh of humans as He does someone that is Spirit-filled. There's a difference between grieving the Spirit and quenching the Spirit. God's people need to know that difference. When God's Spirit is quenched, He no longer operates in the individual. The Spirit still resides in the individual, but it is dormant. God's Spirit remains in a believer until the Day of Redemption and can be reactivated when believers humble themselves, repents, asks the Lord for forgiveness and turns from their wicked ways! The believer still has a chance to see the error of his/her ways and correct his/her life before the Lord returns. When the believer grieves the Spirit, it has an impact on God's Spirit, but only God can tell us how much. The Apostle Paul states in Ephesians 4:30 (NKJV) –"And do not grieve the Holy Spirit of God, by whom you were sealed for the day of redemption." In the Passive Voice, "to be grieved is to be made sorry, to be sorry and/or sorrowful. The Spirit is affected with sadness, cause grief, thrown into sorrow, as well as, offended. What do you do when someone grieves you? You pray for them and try to help them. However, after a while, if the person remains persistent, you push back and let the person do as he/she pleases! Sometimes you still hang around to pick-up the pieces and hopefully save the individual. I believe God's Spirit works the same way.

God gave us the Holy Spirit of promise when we believed in Jesus. He is the guarantor of our inheritance until the redemption of the purchased possession. The Holy Spirit helps the believer to endure and overcome the wiles of Satan, false teachers and ministers, the lust of our flesh, as well as, hardships, sorrows, tribulations, afflictions, and sufferings that must be faced in life. This way, true and faithful believers will have a testimony. As revealed in Revelation 12:11 (NKJV) - "And they overcame him by the blood of the Lamb and by the word of their testimony, and they did not love their lives to the death." God never gives up on us, but there are times when He gives us over to a reprobate mind to do things that should never be done.

"And even as they did not like to retain God in their knowledge, God gave them over to a reprobate mind, to do those things which are not convenient; being filled with all unrighteousness, fornication, wickedness, covetousness, maliciousness; full of envy, murder, debate, deceit, malignity; whisperers,

backbiters, haters of God, despiteful, proud, boasters, inventors of evil things, disobedient to parents, without understanding, covenant breakers, without natural affection, implacable, unmerciful: who knowing the judgment of God, that they which commit such things are worthy of death, not only do the same, but have pleasure in them that do them" Romans 1:28-32 (KJV).

Please remember, "But we have this treasure in earthen vessels that the excellence of the power may be of God and not of us. We are hard-pressed on every side, yet not crushed; we are perplexed, but not in despair; persecuted, but not forsaken; struck down, but not destroyed— always carrying about in the body the dying of the Lord Jesus, that the life of Jesus also may be manifested in our body. For we who live are always delivered to death for Jesus' sake, that the life of Jesus also may be manifested in our mortal flesh. So then death is working in us, but life in you" 2 Corinthians 4:7-12 (NKJV).

Contents

CHAPTER 1

God's Kingdom Suffers Violence!

§

The Wickedness of Sinful Flesh (after the fall)!

Our Lord, Jesus Christ, made it perfectly clear that _only a few_ would find the way to God's Kingdom. It is because of the narrow gate and the difficult way which leads to _life_ in the Kingdom of God! Jesus said, "Enter by the narrow gate; for wide is the gate and broad is the way that leads to destruction, and there are many who go in by it. Because narrow is the gate and difficult is the way which leads to life, and there are few who find it" Matthew 7:13-14 (NKJV). The broad way that leads to destruction signifies an individual's spiritual and eternal perdition (final and irrevocable spiritual ruin). Metaphorically, it refers to men/women that are persistent in doing evil and wicked acts. For those who practice the evil works of the flesh _will not inherit the kingdom of God_. The narrow gate metaphorically means trouble, suffering afflictions or distress through the pressure of circumstances or the antagonism of people we encounter. This requires believers to press hard and to press violently to force one's way into God's Kingdom. In other words, individuals must not _only surrender_ their hearts and their will to Jesus, but they must hunger and thirst for righteousness because it only comes by the Spirit. It is like pressing one's own heart to seek, demand and/or invoke love, faith and obedience to the Lord in order to be transformed to the will of God.

Please know that the way to destruction is a lot easier to travel than entering the narrow gate. One has to _endure_ suffering, afflictions and adversities to enter the narrow (strait) gate to God's Kingdom. This means it takes _more_ effort, patience, endurance and tenacity to enter the Kingdom. *It does not come easy.*

This book defines the true nature of those who *are not* born-again, who are still under the influence of their lustful flesh and satanic powers. It also identifies those who are *true saints* of God, who are faithful and obedient to God's Word. To do this, we have to go back to the garden and follow the _progression of humans_ who were originally created in God's image but were transformed into sinful natured beings (sinful flesh). Revealing the complete nature and characteristics of sinful flesh is extremely important because most Christians do not realize who they were before conversion. Furthermore, few believers rarely examine themselves to see if their faith is genuine or whether they are being obedient to God's Word. "Examine yourselves as to whether you are in the faith. Test yourselves. Do you not know yourselves, that Jesus Christ is in you?—unless indeed you are disqualified. But I trust that you will know that we are not disqualified" 2 Corinthians 13:5-6 (NKJV).

I say this because so many believers (both servants of God and congregants) are spiritually blind. They are unable to see or discern their own faithlessness and disobedience! After reading this book and studying the Scriptures in it, you will find answers to why the world, the church and God's servants are the way they are today! Jesus teachings revealed the spiritual blindness of His followers (the multitude), _who are_ symbolic of today's Christians. He also made know why these individuals were not given to know the mysteries of the Kingdom of heaven like His disciples were. Jesus parables revealed the holiness and the wickedness in the lives of believers who are God's elect that were predestinated and called before the world was formed. He revealed how some are enduring and overcoming Satan and his angels, as well as, the causes of spiritual blindness, deceptions and why many are allow the lust of their flesh to become dominant in their lives! Remember, it is sinful flesh that battles God's Spirit for control of the souls of His people.

Before anything happened on the earth with humans, God blessed those He chose with every spiritual blessing in the heavenly places in

Christ. God's favor continues to occur as God's Spirit invokes blessings upon those who believe and call upon the name of the Lord. It happens to those who surrender themselves to Jesus and to the power of the Holy Spirit to lead and guide them in all truth. These are the individuals who truly seek God's Kingdom, His will and callings in their lives. Because of it, they grow in God's wisdom and knowledge. I would say most Christians believe they are achieving this growth and will receive salvation. However, let me seriously caution you because Jesus reveals that only a few find the way to *life* in God's Kingdom and here's why! How does one tell a blind person to see the things that are righteous which are right before them? Well, it cannot be done without a miracle or the supernatural intervention of God. I hate to say, but there are millions of blinded Christians in the world. They do not see, hear or understand with their hearts the many secrets and mysteries of God. They believe they do, but eternity will reveal the truth! Jesus said, "Therefore I speak to them in parables, because seeing they do not see, and hearing they do not hear, nor do they understand" Matthew 13:13 (NKJV). There is a multitude of spiritually blind Christians today that do not even realize it.

> *"And in them the prophecy of Isaiah is fulfilled, which says: 'Hearing you will hear and shall not understand, and seeing you will see and not perceive; for the hearts of this people have grown dull. Their ears are hard of hearing, and their eyes they have closed, lest they should see with their eyes and hear with their ears, lest they should understand with their hearts and turn, so that I should heal them" Matthew 13:14-15 (NKJV).*

Many believers will read this information and discard the revelation of this word as something that does not apply to them. This is just the way of life and Christianity, so many are spiritually blind! Being blind is being unable to see, examine or judge things. Because the church has a proliferation of false ministers and teachers, the way of truth is not being rendered. Many ministers in the body of Christ are simply entertaining the people and telling them what they want to hear! Many Christians ask, "How can God bless me or when will I receive a harvest?" This causes many of

God's servants to satisfy their itching ears with false doctrine or a doctrine that caters only to the rewarding the flesh! "For the time will come when they will not endure sound doctrine, but according to their own desires, because they have itching ears, they will heap up for themselves teachers; and they will turn their ears away from the truth, and be turned aside to fables" 2 Timothy 4:3-4 (NKJV). A fable is a story, narrative, a fiction of an account in which there is some falsification of truth.

God's people are expected to be *transformed* from their sinful flesh, which resulted from the curse, to Spirit-filled believers guided by God's Spirit. Once a believer belongs to Jesus Christ and begins to live according to the Spirit, he/she is not condemned for sin. The believer belongs to Jesus and God's Spirit has freed him or her from sin (no judgment). "So now there is no condemnation for those who belong to Christ Jesus. And because you belong to him, the power of the life-giving Spirit has freed you from the power of sin that leads to death. The Law of Moses was unable to save us because of the weakness of our sinful nature. So God did what the law could not do. He sent his own Son in a body like the bodies we sinners have. And in that body God declared an end to sin's control over us by giving his Son as a sacrifice for our sins. Jesus fulfilled the requirements of the Law by being obedient to God's Word and despite the suffering in a body like our sinful flesh, He proved His faithfulness. He did this so that the just requirement of the law would be fully satisfied for us, who no longer choose to follow our sinful nature but instead follow the Spirit" Romans 8:1-4 (NLT). However, if the believer willfully sins and continues to practice sin, there no longer remains a sacrifice for his or her sins. "Dear friends, if we deliberately continue sinning after we have received knowledge of the truth, there is no longer any sacrifice that will cover these sins. There is only the terrible expectation of God's judgment and the raging fire that will consume his enemies" Hebrews 10:26-27 (NLT). Every believer should *know* and *understand* this truth!

This, by far, is the greatest blind spot affecting Christians. So many of God's people are not who they think they are! Many proclaim Jesus Christ as the Lord of their lives. They also testify that they love Jesus Christ, have faith in Him and obey God's Word. Yet in reality, very few qualify by the simple requirement set by the Father. Jesus said, "If you love Me, keep My commandments" John 14:15 (NKJV). The word _keep_ means "to observe, to give heed to," as in the keeping of commandments, etc. The word _commandment_ is used of moral and religious precepts. It is a statement of what to do that must be obeyed by those concerned. However, the flesh is weak and falls short of God's will. Furthermore, we are not saved by our works anyway! "He saved us, not because of the righteous things we had done, but because of his mercy. He washed away our sins, giving us a new birth and new life through the Holy Spirit" Titus 3:5 (NLT). Therefore, we _become righteous_ through the power of the Holy Spirit. "For what the law could not do in that it was weak through the flesh, God did by sending His own Son in the likeness of sinful flesh, on account of sin: He condemned sin in the flesh, that the righteous requirement of the law might be fulfilled in us who do not walk according to the flesh but according to the Spirit" Romans 8:3-4 (NKJV).

The Fallen Nature of Humans!

Jesus prophesied the life and times of God's creation at the end of the age before His return. He spoke these things to His disciples regarding the body of Christ. "Then you will be arrested, persecuted, and killed. You will be hated all over the world because you are my followers. And many will turn away from me and betray and hate each other. And many false prophets will appear and will deceive many people. Sin will be rampant everywhere, and the love of many will grow cold. But the one who endures to the end will be saved" Matthew 24:9-13 (NLT). Because of this revelation and truth, we should not be surprised or deceived. Tribulations, false teachings, sorrows, catastrophic events and sufferings will happen both in the world and to those of the household of faith. We see the evidence of these things occurring right now; yet Jesus said "See that you are not troubled; for all these things must come to pass, but the end is not yet. For nation will rise against nation, and kingdom against kingdom. And there will be famines, pestilences, and earthquakes in various places. All these are the beginning of sorrows" Matthew 24:6-8 (NKJV). Now is the time for the church to reveal the truth of God's Kingdom and the violence that opposes God's people. God subjects His creation to vanity as results of their disobedience in the garden. However, it was done in hope that they will overcome this ungodly state. There is hope that the fallen nature of humans will be delivered from the bondage of corruption into the glorious liberty of the children of God. Believers must quickly learn to engage God's Spirit and deny their flesh which desires to follow the world's ways. Part of this end-time problem is the apostasy that is occurring in the church and believers giving way to the lust of the flesh. History repeats itself because the sinful nature of humans continues to be the dominant factor in the war between the flesh and God's Spirit!

The plight a *faithful* Christian is to seek God's Kingdom with all his/her might, heart and soul and press into it! Yes... I said plight because we know that the way which leads to life in God's Kingdom is difficult. Plus, the gate which one must enter is narrow. The Apostle Paul gave meaning to the narrow gate of the Kingdom and the difficult pathway one must travel when he revealed the tribulations we must endure to enter the Kingdom of God. "Strengthening the souls of the disciples, exhorting them to continue in the faith, and saying, "We must through many tribulations enter the kingdom of God" Acts 14:22 (NKJV). Besides, faithful and obedient believers are called to present their bodies to God as a living sacrifice holy and acceptable. "I beseech you therefore, brethren, by the mercies of God, that you present your bodies a living sacrifice, holy, acceptable to God, which is your reasonable service. And do not be conformed to this world, but be transformed by the renewing of your mind, that you may prove what is that good and acceptable and perfect will of God" Romans 12:1-2 (NKJV). Entering God's Kingdom requires a believer to hunger; thirst and have an intense desire to move pass all obstacles in life to become a citizen of the Kingdom.

However, many of God's people have not risen above the desires of their flesh to be delivered from the bondage of corruption into the glorious liberty of the children of God. The situation exists today! Oh, many individuals have become Christians and served in either the church or in ministry. Nevertheless, their hearts were dulled and Satan was able to influence them to seek the things of this world versus the rule and reign of Jesus Christ! The Apostle John explains it this way, "For all that is in the world—the lust of the flesh, the lust of the eyes, and the pride of life—is not of the Father but is of the world" 1 John 2:16 (NKJV). These are the things which defile the mind, heart and soul of humans, even Christians. It is the very reason Jesus says that only a few will find *life* in God's Kingdom.

I feel believers would be better able to serve and to overcome Satan and his angels, if they knew the transformation process that occurred in man as result of Adam and Eve's disobedience in the Garden of Eden. Originally, human beings were created in God's image and likeness. "So God created man in His own image; in the image of God He created him; male and female He created them" Genesis 1:27 (NKJV). They were Spirit-filled beings who were in perfect harmony with God. Once they ate the fruit from the forbidden tree, they took on a sinful nature. Most believers know that we all sin and fall short of God's glory, but do God's people understand that there are only two ways to live on this earth? Humans transform themselves by the renewing of their mind to the image and likeness of Jesus as born-again believers in the Kingdom of God or they remain as sinful-natured creatures of this world submitting themselves to the god of this world, Satan!

Humankind's *sinful nature* is known as operating/living in the flesh according to the carnal mind. This is the reason the flesh and the Spirit war daily to take control of the soul. "I say then: Walk in the Spirit, and you shall not fulfill the lust of the flesh. For the flesh lusts against the Spirit and the Spirit against the flesh; and these are contrary to one another, so that you do not do the things that you wish" Galatians 5:16-17 (NKJV).

What then is sinful nature of flesh and how does it affect the character and behavior of humans? The flesh (human's sinful nature), denotes mere human nature, the earthly nature of man apart from divine influence, and therefore prone to sin and opposed to God. Attempting to understand the flesh, its sinful nature and the transformation it must go through to be saved is very important. Every believer should inquire about this dynamic, especially those called by God as servants. Humans may go through several transformations during the course of their lives. Hopefully, your final transformation or spiritual behavior before the Lord will be Spirit-filled, holy and acceptable to the Lord. For it is humankind's *final* character state and/or behavior that determines whether they enter God's eternal Kingdom!

We all know the Scripture regarding our salvation. "For God so loved the world that He gave His only begotten Son, that whoever believes in Him should not perish but have everlasting life" John 3:16 (NKJV). This is the short version regarding salvation because inheriting eternal life has many component parts. One must be born-again and living according to God's Spirit as an example of what must accompany our belief in Jesus. "Jesus answered, "Most assuredly, I say to you, unless one is born of water and the Spirit, he cannot enter the kingdom of God. That which is born of the flesh is flesh and that which is born of the Spirit is spirit" John 3:5-6 (NKJV). Hopefully, humankind's final transformation, at Christ's return, is Spirit-filled believer!

As you read and understand the transformation of humans from the Garden of Eden until the end of the age, please understand that many were called to attend the final wedding feast of the Lamb, but in the end, only a few were chosen! "For many are called, but few are chosen" Matthew 22:14 (NKJV). The parable of the wedding feast reveals that all did not wear the required wedding garment which is a *coat of righteousness*. This clearly reveals that all of God's people will not be saved nor will they transform into the character of Jesus Christ during their season on the earth. Many believe they will be saved, but not so! It is because their *flesh* becomes the dominant force in their lives. Living according to the flesh with the carnal mind makes even believers open to the influences of Satan and his demons. Desiring the riches of this world and those things which pleasure the flesh chokes out God's Word and His Spirit; therefore the Word of God becomes unfruitful in their lives. "And the cares of this world, the deceitfulness of riches, and the desires for other things entering in choke the word, and it becomes unfruitful" Mark 4:19 (NKJV).

So how and why does the flesh (sinful nature) become so dominant in the life of humans, even Christians? This transformation is better understood as we reveal the plight of humans from the garden up to current life. It all began with the curse of man!

"Then the Lord God took the man and put him in the Garden of Eden to tend and keep it. And the Lord God commanded the man, saying, "Of every tree of the garden you may freely eat; but of the tree of the knowledge of good and evil you shall not eat, for in the day that you eat of it you shall surely die" Genesis 2:15-17 (NKJV).

Then to Adam He said, "Because you have heeded the voice of your wife, and have eaten from the tree of which I commanded you, saying, 'You shall not eat of it': "Cursed is the ground for your sake; in toil you shall eat of it all the days of your life. Both thorns and thistles it shall bring forth for you, and you shall eat the herb of the field. In the sweat of your face you shall eat bread till you return to the ground, for out of it you were taken; for dust you are, and to dust you shall return" Genesis 3:17-19 (NKJV).

It does not take a rocket scientist to see that the things God freely gave us before sin were taken away and now all humanity must endure the trials, tribulations, afflictions, sorrows, hardships, chastisements and sufferings of this life until we enter God's Kingdom. In the Kingdom of God, faithful believers enjoy a tranquil life of God's peace, joy and happiness. Furthermore, the endurance we must endure is _for our sake_. Endurance is part of a Divine purpose of God to redeem His chosen people as worthy sons and daughters. In the fullness of time, God's promise of a Savior (Jesus Christ) came forth to redeem those He predestined and called before the world was formed. "Even so we, when we were children, we _were in bondage under the elements of the world_. But when the fullness of the time had come, God sent forth His Son, born of a woman, born under the law, to redeem those who were under the law, that we might receive the adoption as sons" Galatians 4:3-5 (NKJV).

God's Planned Purpose on Earth!

All life began in the heart of God and was *predestined* according to His purposes on earth. Not many understand the predestination process God set forth because of conflicting research, analyses and reports. Many spiritual leaders have difficulty agreeing on what it is and/or whether it even exists! Hopefully, with the following insight from God's Word, you will more clearly understand God's Divine will regarding predestination.

God's Foreknowledge and Purposes of His Creation!

Telling you that God is all powerful and all-knowing is not revealing anything you do not already know, but it is worth saying again for the purpose of this discussion. God is **omnipotent** which is having unlimited power or authority. He is **omnificent** which is creating all things; having unlimited powers of creation and He is **omniscient** which is having total knowledge; knowing everything. God's **omnipresence** is being present everywhere simultaneously. To be totally honest, human words cannot express or define the fullness, power and authority of God because He is everything we know and more! I say this to explain that *before* God created the heavens and the earth, He foreknew His creation. He also predestined and called those He foreknew.

Yes, God foreknew His creation before He formed the earth and all therein. He knew the hearts and the tendencies of all who would be born on earth. He not only predestined us, but He *called* us for His Divine purpose. God desired to adopt children. Isn't it an awesome thing to know that our creator foreknew every individual to be born in such an intimate way?

"And we know that all things work together for good to those who love God, to those who are the called according to His purpose. For whom He foreknew, He also predestined to be conformed to the image of His Son, that He might be the firstborn among many brethren. Moreover whom He predestined, these He also called; whom He called, these He also justified; and whom He justified, and these He also glorified" Romans 8:28-30 (NKJV).

Whom He called, He justified and glorified that we should be holy and without blame before Him. God had a plan for our lives even before we were born. Now we can see God's omnipotence, His omnificence and omniscience in action. God told Jeremiah that He knew him before He formed him in his mother's womb. God sanctified him and ordained him a prophet before Jeremiah took his first breath as a little baby. "Then the word of the LORD came to me, saying: "Before I formed you in the womb I knew you; before you were born I sanctified you; I ordained you a prophet to the nations" Jeremiah 1:4-5 (NKJV). God foreknew us the same way! He predestined and ordained our lives for His Divine purpose as He did Jeremiah's. Yet, in all of this, He gave humans free-will and/or free choice in life! There are numerous individuals called by God to do a special work, i.e. ministry of some kind, who have never matured or accepted God's calling because of their unrighteous living.

As I mentioned earlier, a lot of theologians have gotten a little confused regarding the predestination of God's people. Some Bible scholars have a problem with the meaning and execution of predestination. The meaning of the word *predestine* is to decree or determine beforehand; to foreordain by divine will or decree. They believe predestination flies in the face of humankind's free-will which is unfair! Some of them tend to believe predestination means that God determines beforehand who will be saved and who will not. Because of this misunderstanding, many people believe humans do not have free-will to choose salvation even if they are righteous before God. They contend that if God chooses to save some of His people and not all means He is not being fair to those who are not chosen who don't have a relationship with him). Theologians' belief in this instance undermines the free will of God's people? There is some degree of truth in their analyses; however, I must say, they do not have the full revelation of God's predestination. Nonetheless, the truth is found in the Bible.

God's plan for His people is fair and complete! The result of human deliverance and salvation is totally up to faithful believers. For those whom God foreknew, believers, they have the ability through the power of God's Spirit to become righteous before Him. They must, of course, live according to the Spirit and the full counsel of His Word! See God's full plan below:

"Blessed be the God and Father of our Lord Jesus Christ, who has blessed us with every spiritual blessing in the heavenly places in Christ, just as He chose

us in Him before the foundation of the world, that we should be holy and without blame before Him in love, having predestined us to adoption as sons by Jesus Christ to Himself, according to the good pleasure of His will, to the praise of the glory of His grace, by which He made us accepted in the Beloved.

In Him we have redemption through His blood, the forgiveness of sins, according to the riches of His grace which He made to abound toward us in all wisdom and prudence, having made known to us the mystery of His will, according to His good pleasure which He purposed in Himself, that in the dispensation of the fullness of the times He might gather together in one all things in Christ, both which are in heaven and which are on earth—in Him. In Him also we have obtained an inheritance, being predestined according to the purpose of Him who works all things according to the counsel of His will that we who first trusted in Christ should be to the praise of His glory.

"In Him you also trusted, after you heard the word of truth, the gospel of your salvation; in whom also, having believed, you were sealed with the Holy Spirit of promise, who is the guarantee of our inheritance until the redemption of the purchased possession, to the praise of His glory" Ephesians 1:3-14 (NKJV).

The success of God's plan for humans is dependent on the free-will choices of believers! God blessed us with every spiritual blessing in the heavenly places in Christ, before the world was made in order for humans to fulfill His will. Therefore, humankind has everything _needed_ to be redeemed and saved. . The choice to fulfill God's plan has always been given to faithful believers. Humankind's obedience, love and faithfulness to God, the Father and to His Son, Jesus Christ, are mandatory as faithful saints. As Scripture reveals, humanity has continuously made poor choices in their commitment to the Lord from one generation to the next. God's people have become slaves to their flesh, to the corruption of this world and to the wiles (cunning devices, methods and the craft of deceit) of Satan. God's hope is "that all come to such unity in our faith and knowledge of God's Son that we will mature in the Lord, measuring up to the full and complete standard of Christ" Ephesians 4:13 (NLT). Also, that our eyes are opened to see the hope of God's calling and that we are delivered from the bondage of corruption! "The eyes of your understanding being enlightened; that you may know what is the hope of His calling, what are the riches of the glory of His inheritance in the saints, and what is the exceeding greatness of His power toward us who believe, according to the working of His mighty power" Ephesians 1:18-19 (NKJV).

Understanding the Truth of God's Predestination and Calling!

As stated before, to understand predestination, you must understand God's foreknowledge of His creation. As revealed in Scripture above, "For whom He foreknew, He also predestined to be conformed to the image of His Son, that He might be the firstborn among many brethren. Moreover whom He predestined, these He also called" Romans 8:29-30 (NKJV). God in all of His infinite wisdom foreknew His people, their hearts and their tendencies before He created the world. This insight is validated in Scripture. "Men of Israel, hear these words: Jesus of Nazareth, a Man attested by God to you by miracles, wonders, and signs which God did through Him in your midst, as you yourselves also know—Him, being delivered by the *determined purpose and foreknowledge* of God, you have taken by lawless hands, have crucified, and put to death; whom God raised up, having loosed the pains of death, because it was not possible that He should be held by it" Acts 2:22-24 (NKJV). God foreknew what would happen. He foreknew that His chosen people (the Jews) would reject the Savior. His prearranged plan was carried out when Jesus was betrayed. He also foreknew that Adam and Eve would be disobedient to his command in the Garden of Eden. God knows everything just like He knows that most of His people are rejecting Him by their ungodly actions today. I realize that many of these individuals are Christians, but there are big differences in one saying that they love Jesus and are obedient to God's Word and actually *doing it!*

Even though God foreknew the hearts of His people would be continuously evil, He still predestined, called, justified and glorified His elect. God proclaimed the evilness of His creation's heart in Genesis. "Then the LORD saw that the wickedness of man was great in the earth, and that every intent of the thoughts of his heart was only evil continually. And the LORD was sorry that He had made man on the earth, and He was grieved in His heart" Genesis 6:5-6 (NKJV). You should ask yourself why God would make this statement when He already foreknew the hearts of the people. The truth of the matter is God knew the vastness of their evil hearts, but we, His people, did not! He let us know how massive the problem is! God's reference to the evilness of the people's heart refers to His entire creation and not just a group of people. Many times God's people read His Word and believe everything in it applies to someone else. Well, this is a caution! So do not get-up on your pompous horse and think God is referring to someone else. Remember, "For all have sinned and fall short of the glory of God" Romans 3:23 (NKJV). If it was not for God's love and grace, none of us would be saved. As faithful believers, we must constantly examine ourselves and our faith.

As you now know, there are those who believe predestination means that God determines beforehand who will be saved and who will not. However, that is not the case at all. God has control over His creation. Those whom God foreknew, He *predestined* and *called*. It is God, our Creator, who decides to whom He will show mercy and compassion. He likewise decides whose heart should be hardened. We are mere sinful flesh who is in no position to decide or challenge God's justice! It is God who decides how we should be created.

Are we saying, then, that God was unfair? Of course not! For God said to Moses, "I will show mercy to anyone I choose, and I will show compassion to anyone I choose." So it is God who decides to show mercy. We can neither choose it nor work for it. For the Scriptures say that God told Pharaoh, "I have appointed you for the very purpose of displaying my power in you and to spread my fame throughout the earth." So you see, God chooses to show mercy to some, and he chooses to harden the hearts of others so they refuse to listen.

Well then, you might say, "Why does God blame people for not responding? Haven't they simply done what he makes them do?" No, don't say that. Who are you, a mere human being, to argue with God? Should the thing that was created say to the one who created it, "Why have you made me like this?" When a potter makes jars out of clay, doesn't he have a right to use the same lump of clay to make one jar for decoration and another to throw garbage into? In the same way, even though God has the right to show his anger and his power, he is very patient with those on whom his anger falls, who are destined for destruction. He does this to make the riches of his glory shine even brighter on those to whom he shows mercy, who were prepared in advance for glory" Romans 9:14-23 (NLT).

No one should be alarmed regarding God's justice, His predestination and callings because they are more than fair. God sets forth the spiritual area in which humans make their own choices in life. First, you need to understand that God predestined and called *many* before the world was formed. I said He called *many!* However, the choosing faithful believers for salvation part comes after humans have lived on the earth and had their opportunity become faithful and righteous beings, conformed to the image of Jesus Christ. "So the last will be first, and the first last. "For many are called, but few chosen" Matthew 20:16 (NKJV). The definition for the word *many* is a great number! It amounts to or consists of a large *indefinite* number. Indefinite means it is without exact limits: indeterminate. Now, the word *call* is to call anyone, invite or summon. It is used particularly of the Divine call to partake of the blessings of redemption. The call by God is to be invited (by God in the proclamation of the Gospel) to obtain eternal salvation in the kingdom through Christ. Therefore, the issue is *not in the calling* because an indefinite number was called before God created the world, *the issue is being chosen!* Scripture has it that only a *few will be chosen!* The ones Jesus will select are those who become worthy sons and daughters. These are God's elect, faithful believers.

If you are a believer, you are one of the ones called of God. The calling occurs when the Holy Spirit reveals God's grace and salvation to us. He also instructs us to turn from godless living and sinful pleasures. "For the grace of God has been revealed, bringing salvation to all people. And we are instructed to turn from godless living and sinful pleasures. We should live in this evil world with wisdom, righteousness, and devotion to God, while we look forward with hope to that wonderful day when the glory of our great God and Savior, Jesus Christ, will be revealed. He gave his life to free us from every kind of sin, to cleanse us, and to make us his very own people, totally committed to doing good deeds" Titus 2:11-14 (NLT). However, being called of God does not mean you will be chosen. Being chosen *only* comes to those who love Jesus and are faithful to Him and are obedient to God's Word.

You may be asking the question, why would God call His people if He foreknew that most of them would fail to become faithful and obedient. That question was answered by the Apostle Paul. He revealed, "For the creation was subjected to futility [vanity], not willingly, but because of Him who subjected it in hope; because the creation itself also will be delivered from the bondage of corruption into the glorious liberty of the children of God" Romans 8:20-21 (NKJV). God called His elect in hopes that they would be delivered from the bondage of corruption into the glorious liberty of the children of God. Paul further reminded us that the sufferings of this present time; our lives on earth will be no way compared to the glory which shall be revealed in us. "For I consider that the sufferings of this present time are not worthy to be compared with the glory which shall be revealed in us. For the earnest expectation of the creation eagerly waits for the revealing of the sons of God" Romans 8:18-19 (NKJV).

There are many parts to God's predestination plan ordained by Him to be consummated on earth in the fullness of God's time. "For we are His workmanship, created in Christ Jesus for good works, which God prepared beforehand that we should walk in them" Ephesians 2:10 (NKJV). The word *ordained* means to determine the fate of in advance; to predetermine, decide beforehand. God *foreknew* the disobedience and rejection of His special, the Jewish nation; therefore He predestined His Son, Jesus Christ as the Savior of the world. God also predestined those He foreknew whose heart was willing and would be acceptable to His calling. It did not mean they would fulfill God's will completely, but that they were good candidates for salvation. Hopefully, these individuals would be delivered from the bondage of corruption by the power of the Holy Spirit. Those who believe in Jesus will be sealed with the Holy Spirit of promise who guarantees their inheritance until the redemption of the purchased possession It then becomes a matter of the believer walking and living according to the leading of God's Spirit!

"In Him we have redemption through His blood, the forgiveness of sins, according to the riches of His grace which He made to abound toward us in all wisdom and prudence, having made known to us the mystery of His will, according to His good pleasure which He purposed in Himself, that in the dispensation of the fullness of the times He might gather together in one all things in Christ, both which are in heaven and which are on earth— in Him. In Him also we have obtained an inheritance, being predestined according to the purpose of Him who works all things according to the counsel of His will that we who first trusted in Christ should be to the praise of His glory.

In Him you also trusted, after you heard the word of truth, the gospel of your salvation; in whom also, having believed, you were sealed with the Holy Spirit of promise, who is the guarantee of our inheritance until the redemption of the purchased possession, to the praise of His glory" Ephesians 1:7-14 (NKJV).

We know that God works all things together for those who would truly love Him and His Son, Jesus Christ. For those God *foreknew* He *predestined* to conform to the image and likeness of Jesus. Those God foreknew He called. He also *justified* them, which is giving them right standing with Himself. Also, God *glorified* those He called and justified. Being glorified is giving them His glory. It is the state of blessedness into which believers are to enter hereafter being brought into the likeness of Christ.

"And we know that all things work together for good to those who love God, to those who are the called according to His purpose. For whom He foreknew, He also predestined to be conformed to the image of His Son, that He might be the firstborn among many brethren. Moreover whom He predestined, these He also called; whom He called, these He also justified; and whom He justified, and these He also glorified" Romans 8:28-30 (NKJV).

17

As you can see, God's predestination and calling consecrates (dedicate solemnly to a service or goal) believers to the point of their free-will. The free-will of humans allows them to make their choices in life whether to serve God or serve their flesh (which is influenced by the god of this world). From the point of your calling, the choice of life is totally up to you. God has done all the work He needs to do. His work was finished when He created the heavens and the earth. "So the creation of the heavens and the earth and everything in them was completed. On the seventh day God had finished his work of creation, so he rested from all his work" Genesis 2:1-2 (NLT). Jesus finished His work when He died on the Cross. "So when Jesus had received the sour wine, He said, "It is finished!" And bowing His head, He gave up His spirit" John 19:30 (NKJV). Everything else is set forth to occur *spiritually* in the fullness of God's time!

Therefore, God ordained everything to occur in His predestination process. The completion of God's adoption process, which is fulfillment, is totally dependent upon you fulfilling God's will on earth. The fulfillment process would not be easy because God's Kingdom suffers violence in many different ways. Listed below are a few of the spiritual dynamics you must learn and do as component parts of your spiritual development and growth to achieve salvation.

- *Know that your body becomes the temple of God's Spirit* - "Do you not know that your body is the temple of the Holy Spirit who is in you, whom you have from God, and you are not your own" 1 Corinthians 6:19 (NKJV)?
- *Understand that you now belong to God and not to yourself* - "For you were bought at a price; therefore glorify God in your body and in your spirit, which are God's" 1 Corinthians 6:20 (NKJV).
- *The flesh and the carnal mind are enemies to God and cannot please Him* – "For those who live according to the flesh set their minds on the things of the flesh, but those who live according to the Spirit, the things of the Spirit. For to be carnally minded is death, but to be spiritually minded is life and peace. Because the carnal mind is enmity against God; for it is not subject to the law of God,

nor indeed can be. So then, those who are in the flesh cannot please God" Romans 8:5-8 (NKJV).

- *You have no obligation to the flesh* – "Therefore, brethren, we are debtors—not to the flesh, to live according to the flesh. For if you live according to the flesh you will die; but if by the Spirit you put to death the deeds of the body, you will live" Romans 8:12-13 (NKJV).

- *Crucify the flesh and its lustful desires* – "And those who are Christ's have crucified the flesh with its passions and desires" Galatians 5:24 (NKJV).

- *Live according to God's Spirit* – "For what the law could not do in that it was weak through the flesh, God did by sending His own Son in the likeness of sinful flesh, on account of sin: He condemned sin in the flesh, that the righteous requirement of the law might be fulfilled in us who do not walk according to the flesh but according to the Spirit." Romans 8:3-4 (NKJV). "For if you live according to the flesh you will die; but if by the Spirit you put to death the deeds of the body, you will live" Romans 8:13 (NKJV).

- *Do not harden your heart and become spiritually blind, unable to hear and commune with God's Spirit* - Jesus said, "And in them the prophecy of Isaiah is fulfilled, which says: 'Hearing you will hear and shall not understand, and seeing you will see and not perceive; for the hearts of this people have grown dull" Matthew 13:14-15 (NKJV).

- *Do not grieve the Spirit* – "And do not grieve the Holy Spirit of God, by whom you were sealed for the day of redemption" Ephesians 4:30 (NKJV).

- *Quench not the Holy Spirit* – "Do not quench the Spirit" Thessalonians 5:19 (NKJV).

- *Be led by the Holy Spirit* – "For the flesh lusts against the Spirit and the Spirit against the flesh; and these are contrary to one another, so that you do not do the things that you wish. But if you are led by the Spirit, you are not under the law" Galatians 5:17-18 (NKJV). "For as many as are led by the Spirit of God, these are sons of God" Romans 8:14 (NKJV).

- *Conform to the image and likeness of Jesus Christ* – "Jesus servants, apostles, prophets, evangelists, pastors and teachers are responsible for equipping God's people to do His work and building up the church, the body of Christ. This will continue until we all come to such unity in our faith and knowledge of God's Son that we will be mature in the Lord, measuring up to the full and complete standard of Christ" Ephesians 4:12-13 (NLT).

- *Understand that God's Kingdom suffers violence* – The Kingdom of God encounters many challenges that were set-forth to <u>test</u> the faith and endurance of those God foreknew and predestined to adopt as sons and daughters. John the Baptist realized this when He faced the antagonism of the scribes and the Pharisees. "And from the days of John the Baptist until now the kingdom of heaven suffers violence, and the violent take it by force" Matthew 11:12 (NKJV). God's people must endure many different trials and challenges as part of their walk with the Holy Spirit and their desire to enter God's Kingdom as follows:

  o All of God's elect should know and understand that as part of Jesus' Body, believers must undergo and endure the sufferings of Christ. As Christ suffered, so shall His Body (the body of Christ). The Apostle Paul gave some comfort to the church at Corinth regarding the suffering they must endure.

  "Blessed be the God and Father of our Lord Jesus Christ, the Father of mercies and God of all comfort, who comforts us in all our tribulation that we may be able to comfort those who are in any trouble, with the comfort with which we ourselves are comforted by God. For as the sufferings of Christ abound in us, so our consolation also abounds through Christ. Now if we are afflicted, it is for your consolation and salvation, which is effective for enduring the same sufferings which we also suffer. Or if we are comforted, it is for your consolation and salvation" 2 Corinthians 1:3-6 (NKJV)

- The sufferings that Christians must endure are: misfortune, calamity, evils and afflictions. Also the afflictions which Christians must undergo are for same causes that Christ patiently endured. For the more we suffer for Christ, the more God will shower us with his comfort through Christ. When you are afflicted, it is for your consolation and salvation.

  o *Trials show that our faith is genuine* – "So be truly glad. There is wonderful joy ahead, even though you must endure many trials for a little while. These trials will show that your faith is genuine. It is being tested as fire tests and purifies gold— though your faith is far more precious than mere gold. So when your faith remains strong through many trials, it will bring you much praise and glory and honor on the day when Jesus Christ is revealed to the whole world. You love him even though you have never seen him. Though you do not see him now, you trust him; and you rejoice with a glorious, inexpressible joy. The reward for trusting him will be the salvation of your souls" 1 Peter 1:6-9 (NLT).

  o *Suffering for God's glory* – "Beloved, do not think it strange concerning the fiery trial which is to try you, as though some strange thing happened to you; but rejoice to the extent that you partake of Christ's sufferings, that when His glory is revealed, you may also be glad with exceeding joy. If you are reproached for the name of Christ, blessed are you, for the Spirit of glory and of God rests upon you. On their part He is blasphemed, but on your part He is glorified" 1 Peter 4:12-14 (NKJV).

  o *Our present suffering cannot not compare to the Glory to be revealed in us* - "For I consider that the sufferings of this present time are not worthy to be compared with the glory which shall be revealed in us" Romans 8:18 (NKJV).

  o *Many false prophets, teachers and ministers will invade the household of faith* – "But there were also false prophets in Israel, just as there will be false teachers among you. They will cleverly teach destructive heresies and even deny the Master who bought them. In this way, they will bring sudden destruction on themselves. Many will follow their evil teaching and shameful immorality. And because of these teachers, the way of truth will be slandered. In their greed they will make up clever lies to get hold of your money. But God condemned them long ago, and their destruction will not be delayed" 2 Peter 2:1-3 (NLT).

o   *Those who endure to the end will be saved* – Jesus said, "Then they will deliver you up to tribulation and kill you, and you will be hated by all nations for My name's sake. And then many will be offended, will betray one another, and will hate one another. Then many false prophets will rise up and deceive many. And because lawlessness will abound, the love of many will grow cold. But he who endures to the end shall be saved" Matthew 24:9-13 (NKJV).

This has been truth of God's predestination, calling and life experiences for those He foreknew before the world was made. God's Word, the Bible, reveals the truth of God's will and the difficulties His people will encounter fulfilling it. Every believer will have to press beyond these difficulties and obstacles in order to be saved. God's Kingdom does *suffer violence*, but the *violent takes the Kingdom by force*. True and faithful believers let nothing stop them because they have learned how to profit from the trials. "My brethren, count it all joy when you fall into various trials, knowing that the testing of your faith produces patience. But let patience have its perfect work, that you may be perfect and complete, lacking nothing" James 1:2-4 (NKJV).

God's People continue to live as Wicked and Sinful Flesh!

We now know that God subjected His creation to *vanity* in hopes that His people will mature through the power of His Spirit and with the spiritual gifts and blessings He gives. "For the creation was subjected to futility [vanity], not willingly, but because of Him who subjected it in hope; because the creation itself also will be delivered from the bondage of corruption into the glorious liberty of the children of God" Romans 8:20-21 (NKJV). Spiritual gifts, godly wisdom and knowledge, plus spiritual weapons are sufficient to deliver all from the bondage of this world's corruption. Those who do not develop and mature in the things of the Lord, as born-again believers, will remain as *sinful flesh!* Please do not overlook or be deceived regarding this insight! Sinful- natured (flesh) individuals are the ones who travel the road to destruction. There are many people living this way according to the words of Jesus Christ! Because God gave humans *free-will* to make their own choices in life, it is humans who must choose between being faithful, obedient and maturing in the things of God versus remaining in bondage to world. These individuals continue to live in vanity and/or futility throughout their lives on earth. Many of God's people have not followed His eternal plan for their lives, thus history repeats itself over and over again! Instead of being enlightened, many of God's people are forever leaning but never coming to the knowledge of the truth. In fact, *many* church leaders (pastors, ministers, teachers, etc.), as well as congregants are spiritually blind and are unable to see, hear or understand the Word of God's Kingdom nor its mysteries.

The Apostle Paul advised Timothy of deception that God's people would encounter in the last days! "You should know this, Timothy that in the last days there will be very difficult times. For people will love only themselves and their money. They will be boastful and proud, scoffing at God, disobedient to their parents, and ungrateful. They will consider nothing sacred. They will be unloving and unforgiving; they will slander others and have no self-control. They will be cruel and hate what is good. They will betray their friends, be reckless, be puffed up with pride, and love pleasure rather than God. They will act religious, but they will reject the power that could make them godly. Stay away from people like that" 2 Timothy 3:1-5 (NLT).

It is our *heart that defiles us* and the thoughts of the human heart are continually evil. This is why we must experience transformation in our lives and become born-again and please God. It is the only way to become righteous before Him. When believers walk and live according to the Holy Spirit, it indicates that their hearts have been changed by the power of the Spirit. These individuals are now living to become righteous before God and to remove the vanity in their hearts. Jesus encountered a confrontation with the scribes and Pharisees regarding the washing of hands when He identified vanity within their hearts and how defilement comes from within! He shared with them the truth of the human heart, yet they continue to reject His Gospel.

DEFILEMENT COMES FROM WITHIN

Then the scribes and Pharisees who were from Jerusalem came to Jesus, saying, "Why do Your disciples transgress the tradition of the elders? For they do not wash their hands when they eat bread." He answered and said to them, "Why do you also transgress the commandment of God because of your tradition? For God commanded, saying, 'Honor your father and your mother'; and, 'He who curses father or mother, let him be put to death.' But you say, 'Whoever says to his father or mother, "Whatever profit you might have received from me is a gift to God"—then he need not honor his father or mother.' Thus you have made the commandment of God of no effect by your tradition.

Hypocrites! Well did Isaiah prophesy about you, saying: 'These people draw near to Me with their mouth, and honor Me with their lips, but their heart is far from Me. And in vain they worship Me, teaching as doctrines the commandments of men." When He had called the multitude to Himself, He said to them, "Hear and understand: Not what goes into the mouth defiles a man; but what comes out of the mouth, this defiles a man." Then His disciples came and said to Him, "Do You know that the Pharisees were offended when they heard this saying?" But He answered and said, "Every plant which My heavenly Father has not planted will be uprooted. Let them alone. They are blind leaders of the blind. And if the blind leads the blind, both will fall into a ditch."

Then Peter answered and said to Him, "Explain this parable to us." So Jesus said, "Are you also still without understanding? Do you not yet understand that whatever enters the mouth goes into the stomach and is eliminated? But those things which proceed out of the mouth come from the heart, and they defile a man. For out of the heart proceed evil thoughts, murders, adulteries, fornications, thefts, false witness, and blasphemies. These are the things which defile a man, but to eat with unwashed hands does not defile a man" Matthew 15:1-20 (NKJV).

As you can see, our hearts are the utmost and foremost obstacle requiring violent action on our part to press though to God's Kingdom. Our hearts are evil and must be changed by the power of God's Spirit. Please understand that out of the heart proceeds evil thoughts, murders, adulteries, fornications, thefts, false witness and blasphemies. These are the things humans think on! They defile the individual and make them unworthy and unrighteous before the Lord! You may not think about it much, but secretly the human heart is always attempting to get it way and please the flesh of an individual. So, how does one press past the evilness of their heart? How does one take the *Kingdom by force* within their heart and capture/suppress their own evil thoughts? Everything comes by and through God's Spirit. Because these are spiritual battles, only God's Spirit can break us from the bondage of corruption within our hearts.

The Apostle Paul advised the church at Corinth as to how to overcome the strongholds of our hearts and cast arguments, bringing every thought into captivity and every high thing that exalts itself against the knowledge of God within us! Paul said, "For though we walk in the flesh, we do not war according to the flesh. For the weapons of our warfare are not carnal but mighty in God for pulling down strongholds (those things in which mere human confidence is imposed), casting down arguments and every high thing that exalts itself against the knowledge of God, bringing every thought into captivity to the obedience of Christ, and being ready to punish all disobedience when your obedience is fulfilled" 2 Corinthians 10:3-6 (NKJV). This is the first and foremost line of defense in our battle against the evil thoughts of our mind and heart! To cast down or pull down by force means to destroy completely! Please understand that the power of God's Spirit gives the individual the willingness and ability to pull down and destroy those unwanted thoughts of the hearts. Allowing evil thoughts to exist and build within the heart of an individual leads even a believer to sin!

The battle to be righteous occurs in the hearts of God's people! Sin comes from the heart. "But each one is tempted when he is drawn away by his own desires and enticed. Then, when desire has conceived, it gives birth to sin; and sin, when it is full-grown, brings forth death" James 1:14-15 (NKJV). It is when a person thinks on and allows their desires, cravings, longings, desire for what is forbidden to grow in their hearts. "Having eyes full of adultery and that cannot cease from sin, enticing unstable souls. They have a heart trained in covetous practices, and are accursed children" 2 Peter 2:14 (NKJV). True believers, who hunger and thirst after righteousness comes to a point in life where they seek God's power to make a change in their lives. This is when they refuse in give in to the deeds of their fleshly lusts. In reality, it is taking the Kingdom of God by force and *pressing into it!* Always remember that God's Kingdom is not something you have to get because… the Kingdom of God is in you!

CHAPTER 2

Why Many Christians will not find the Way to Life!

SPIRITUAL BLINDNESS IS CAUSING MANY TO PERISH!

JESUS SPOKE IN PARABLES TO His followers, the multitude. Parables are the mysteries of the Kingdom of heaven and they reveal the truth of how God's people live on the earth. They also reveal how we should live as God's elect people. It is imperative that every Christian know and understand secrets that were held from the foundation of the world. "All these things Jesus spoke to the multitude in parables; and without a parable He did not speak to them, that it might be fulfilled which was spoken by the prophet, saying: "I will open My mouth in parables; I will utter things kept secret from the foundation of the world" Matthew 13:34-35 (NKJV). To the Jewish nation, they were parables; to today's Christians, they are both parables and prophecies of things that will come into existence!

Jesus clearly revealed the short-comings of God's chosen people, the Jews, as well as future generations in the parables He taught! It is because they were both parables (mysteries) and prophecies. In the parable of the Sower, Jesus gave reasons why even God's elect (Jews and Christians) do not see, hear nor understand the mysteries of the Kingdom. This insight also applies to God's servants, those who are called by God to minister truth to His people. Perhaps, spiritual blindness is the main reason only a few teach the parables of Jesus and the Gospel message!

The Parable of the Sower!

"Then He spoke many things to them in parables, saying: "Behold, a sower went out to sow. And as he sowed, some seed fell by the wayside; and the birds came and

devoured them. Some fell on stony places, where they did not have much earth; and they immediately sprang up because they had no depth of earth. But when the sun was up they were scorched, and because they had no root they withered away. And some fell among thorns, and the thorns sprang up and choked them. But others fell on good ground and yielded a crop: some a hundredfold, some sixty, some thirty. He who has ears to hear, let him hear" Matthew 13:3-9 (NKJV)!

The Purpose of Parables
And the disciples came and said to Him, "Why do You speak to them in parables?" He answered and said to them, "Because it has been given to you to know the mysteries of the kingdom of heaven, but to them it has not been given. For whoever has, to him more will be given, and he will have abundance; but whoever does not have, even what he has will be taken away from him. Therefore I speak to them in parables, because seeing they do not see, and hearing they do not hear, nor do they understand. And in them the prophecy of Isaiah is fulfilled, which says:

'Hearing you will hear and shall not understand, and seeing you will see and not perceive; for the hearts of this people have grown dull. Their ears are hard of hearing, and their eyes they have closed, lest they should see with their eyes and hear with their ears, lest they should understand with their hearts and turn, so that I should heal them" Matthew 13:10-15 (NKJV)!

As an immature Christian, in the early days of my Christian walk, there were many things that I did not understand. I could never understand how so many ministers got involved in adulterous lifestyles when they knew God's Word and its meaning. Furthermore, many of them were involved with other Christians who were equally responsible for being righteous and setting an example as Christians. I also had an issue with the lack of reverence in the house of God. This is the place where parishioners go to hear from God. Right! It is supposed to be holy, yet I have seen so many acts of wickedness in God's house that I wondered why God's Spirit ever visited us. I wondered... where is reverence to God, the fear, honor, holiness and respect? I thought that if God's people read God's Word surely they would know they had violated it.

After the Lord called me to write, He opened my eyes to spiritual blindness and how many of God's people, including those called to minister were spiritually blind! The more I studied God's Word, the more I realized how far from the truth of the Gospel and God's will the church had progressed. God's Spirit spoke to my heart and said, "These individuals may read the same Scriptures you read, but they perceive an entirely different message. Furthermore, many inject their own beliefs from worldly influences and their desires in the messages they give. They teach the commandment of men as doctrine, which is far from the truth. "And in vain they worship Me, teaching *as* doctrines the commandments of men" Matthew 15:9 (NKJV). Their perception is clouded with lust, greed, desire to control and deceitfulness. Hence, they are spiritually blind.

This is especially true for ministers who allow their flesh to dominate them! "But He answered and said, "Every plant which My heavenly Father has not planted will be uprooted. Let them alone. They are blind leaders of the blind. And if the blind leads the blind, both will fall into a ditch" Matthew 15:13-14 (NKJV). This Scripture is similar to Matthew 13:30 (NLT) – "Let both grow together until the harvest. Then I will tell the harvesters to sort out the weeds, tie them into bundles, and burn them and to put the wheat in the barn." Spiritual blindness explains some of the iniquity, corruption, immorality, wickedness and perversion that occur in the household of faith. At that time, I still wondered what caused the blindness in men and women of God, but now I understand because of Jesus teachings.

As I continued to study God's Word and ask Him for wisdom and understanding, He opened my eyes to the transformation which occurred in humans as result of disobedience in the garden. He showed me how the church became infiltrated with people who did not promote God's Kingdom or minister God's full counsel to the body of Christ. At first I was bewildered, but then my heart was saddened when I began to understand the ungodly plight of some of God's people and the saturation of deceitful workers in the church. "These people are false apostles. They are deceitful workers who disguise themselves as apostles of Christ. But I am not surprised! Even Satan disguises himself as an angel of light. So it is no wonder that his servants also disguise themselves as servants of righteousness. In the end they will get the punishment their wicked deeds deserve" 2 Corinthians 11:13-15 (NLT).

False prophets, false ministers, deceitful workers and ungodly people exist in churches all over the world. Even though most of God's people know this situation is real and prevalent in God's house, few are willing to take a stand or identify the truth of the matter. It is because of the friendships that have been developed between God's servants and God's people. A lot of people choose not to *rock the boat* while others choose not to offend leadership. Many just remain in the church and turn their heads away from this wickedness. It is a sad thing for good Christian people to stay in a church even when they know they are not being fed the truth of God's Word. Also, many still stay where there are adulterous situations with leadership and where the people are being entertained, instead of being developed in the things of God. This is one of the reasons that God's people must *press their way* into God's Kingdom by studying The Word for themselves. The Holy Spirit will lead and guide parishioners the way in which they should go! The Apostle Peter spoke truth to this matter and its dangers. He identified the reality of this issue in the house of God! "But there were also false prophets in Israel, just as there will be false teachers among you. They will cleverly teach destructive heresies and even deny the Master who bought them. In this way, they will bring sudden destruction on themselves. Many will follow their evil teaching and shameful immorality. And because of these teachers, the way of truth will be slandered. In their greed they will make up clever lies to get hold of your money. But God condemned them long ago, and their destruction will not be delayed" 2 Peter 2:1-3 (NLT).

Are you aware that many of today false ministers use the same tactic that Satan used in the Garden of Eden and in the wilderness with Jesus? With Eve, the serpent lured her into disobedience by appealing to her flesh and offering her things that appealed to the desires of her flesh. "Then the serpent said to the woman, "You will not surely die. For God knows that in the day you eat of it your eyes will be opened and you will be like God, knowing good and evil." So when the woman saw that the tree was good for food, that it was pleasant to the eyes, and a tree desirable to make one wise, she took of its fruit and ate. She also gave to her husband with her, and he ate" Genesis 3:4-6 (NKJV). Satan attempted the same routine with Jesus, but to no avail! "Again, the devil took Him up on an exceedingly high mountain, and showed Him all the kingdoms of the world and their glory. And he said to Him, "All these things I will give You if You will fall down and worship me." Then Jesus said to him, "Away with you, Satan! For it is written, 'You shall worship the LORD your God, and Him only you shall serve" Matthew 4:8-10 (NKJV). Many of today's preacher's make fleshly promises. They pack the pews by making promises according to the desires and lust of their flesh. People love to hear about how they are going to be blessed and when they will receive a harvest, even when they have been disobedient to God's Word.

False prophets and teachers cause the people to be spiritually blind because of their failure to minister the full counsel of God's Word. However, God has already revealed His displeasure and what He will do to those destructive workers that defile God's people, the temple of God's Spirit! He has said to His people, "Do you not know that you are the temple of God and that the Spirit of God dwells in you? If anyone defiles the temple of God, God will _destroy_ him. For the temple of God is holy, which temple you are" 1 Corinthians 3:16-17 (NKJV). My concern is still for God's people. Because of false teaching, many people will be left by the wayside of life and never come to the knowledge of the truth. God people must become as wise as the serpent. "Behold, I send you out as sheep in the midst of wolves. Therefore be wise as serpents and harmless as doves. But beware of men, for they will deliver you up to councils and scourge you in their synagogues" Matthew 10:16-17 (NKJV).

I realize this is not an easy matter to discuss or reveal (uncover), but we must if we are to become mature Christians. Keep in mind; we are talking about the _salvation_ of many believers. Scripture clearly speaks to it and when we read the words of Jesus Christ, the Apostle Paul and apostles, they make known the iniquity in God's house. In order to provide a clear and complete understanding of _spiritual blindness_ and how it has contaminated the hearts of God's people, I will further explain the results of God's curse of man and the free-will of humans.

FREE-WILL RESULTS IN THE SINFUL NATURE OF HUMANS!

Before the world was formed, God chose His people to be holy and without blame before Him in love, having predestined us to adoption as sons by Jesus Christ to Himself, according to the good pleasure of His will. "Blessed be the God and Father of our Lord Jesus Christ, who has blessed us with every spiritual blessing in the heavenly places in Christ, just as He chose us in Him before the foundation of the world, that we should be holy and without blame before Him in love, having predestined us to adoption as sons by Jesus Christ to Himself, according to the good pleasure of His will, to the praise of the glory of His grace, by which He made us accepted in the Beloved" Ephesians 1:3-4 (NKJV). However, in the garden, God gave man free-will to choose and to do as he pleased. The Lord God cautioned the man regarding his punishment for violating His Word and direction, yet He still gave him the choice to do as he chose to do!

Doing as we pleased meant humanity would become sinful natured creatures whose hearts were consistently evil. The important thing to know as God's people is that we remain in this sinful condition *(sinful flesh)* when we live according to the carnal mind, *until* we become born-again by God's Spirit. God's creation became slaves to sin and corruption as result of man's disobedient in the garden. "Do you not know that to whom you present yourselves slaves to obey, you are that one's slaves whom you obey, whether of sin leading to death, or of obedience leading to righteousness" Romans 6:16 (NKJV)? Believers can be slaves to sin, which leads to death, or they can choose to obey God, which leads to righteous living. Even as Christians, we continue in this unworthy state if we do not live according to God's Spirit. After some believers become born-again they *quench* God's Spirit, due to their sinful acts and deeds, and return to being a slave to sin. "Do not quench the Spirit. Do not despise prophecies.

Test all things; hold fast what is good. Abstain from every form of evil" Thessalonians 5:19-22 (NKJV).

EVILNESS OF THE HEART CAUSES SPIRITUAL BLINDNESS AND LACK OF KNOWLEDGE!

After man was removed from the Garden of Eden and developed a family, the earth began to see the effects of God's curse on human life. Adam and Eve bore two sons, Cain and Abel. While in the garden, Eve was disobedient to God's Word by gratifying the lust of flesh and eating fruit from the forbidden tree. Her oldest son took on an evil spirit of anger and killed his younger brother, as revealed in Genesis.

CAIN MURDERS ABEL

"Now Adam knew Eve his wife, and she conceived and bore Cain, and said, "I have acquired a man from the Lord." Then she bore again, this time his brother Abel. Now Abel was a keeper of sheep, but Cain was a tiller of the ground. And in the process of time it came to pass that Cain brought an offering of the fruit of the ground to the Lord. Abel also brought of the firstborn of his flock and of their fat. And the Lord respected Abel and his offering, but He did not respect Cain and his offering. And Cain was very angry, and his countenance fell.

So the Lord said to Cain, "Why are you angry? And why has your countenance fallen? If you do well, will you not be accepted? And if you do not do well, sin lies at the door. And its desire is for you, but you should rule over it. Now Cain talked with Abel his brother; and it came to pass, when they were in the field, that Cain rose up against Abel his brother and killed him. Then the Lord said to Cain, "Where is Abel your brother?"

He said, "I do not know. Am I my brother's keeper?" And He said, "What have you done? The voice of your brother's blood cries out to Me from the ground. So now you are cursed from the earth, which has opened its mouth to receive your brother's blood from your hand. When you till the ground, it shall no longer yield its strength to you. A fugitive and a vagabond you shall be on the earth" Genesis 4:1-12 (NKJV).

As we can see, the issue with Cain was his *heart*. Cain did not have a willing heart to glorify God with the multitude of his first fruit. Plus, he had evil thoughts towards his brother when his brother gave plenty of his first fruit to God. Cain's evil thoughts turned into anger which later conceived the will to kill his brother, Abel. Because humans became slaves to the bondage to corruption, the wickedness of the human heart became great on the earth. The human heart continues to have evil thoughts even today! The human heart yields greed, selfishness, vanity, pride, ambitions, control and many more disobedient behaviors. Equally as bad is the *inability to see* and *discern* the evilness of one's heart. As people of God, we know how to ask for forgiveness and blessings, but many of us find it difficult to examine and *see the deeds* of our own heart.

The Bible addresses the heart in one way or another 926 times. God's people have received cautions, warnings, truth and spiritual directions regarding the heart from Jesus Christ and all the apostles, yet it remains the source of deception, greed, pride, selfishness and more! Because of the evilness of the thoughts of man's heart, God was sorry He ever made man. "Then the LORD saw that the wickedness of man was great in the earth, and that every intent of the thoughts of his heart was only evil continually. And the LORD was sorry that He had made man on the earth, and He was grieved in His heart" Genesis 6:5-6 (NKJV). Please do not look at others and wonder if their hearts are evil, just look in the mirror and ask God for deliverance. We all need deliverance from our evil hearts and only the power of God's Spirit can accommodate our request!

From the results of God's curse, humanity became vain and futile. "For the creation was made subject to vanity (futility)" Romans 8:20 (KJV). Therefore, all humanity became *vain*. Because the battle to love, maintain faithfulness and be obedient to God and Jesus Christ is in the *heart*, many believers have a hard time overcoming the deeds of it. The deeds of the heart are given to *vanity* and temptation to satisfying our flesh before serving the Lord. The heart is the place where life and death occurs. We know the physical heart is the chambered, muscular organ in the chest; it pumps blood received from the veins, into the arteries and it maintains the flow of blood through the entire circulatory system. However, the heart is also the center of all physical and spiritual life. It encompasses the soul or mind and it is the fountain and seat of the thoughts, passions, desires, appetites, affections, purposes, endeavors. The heart is also the faculty and seat of the intelligence of the will and character of humans.

So, what caused man's heart to have evil thoughts? Why is he motivated to do wrong and be disobedient to the will of God? For that, let us review the human action in the garden. Instead of Eve following God's instructions, she allowed herself to be deceived by the serpent. The serpent was able to deceive Eve because of the thoughts of her heart. Eve became full of vanity by talking to the serpent regarding the things she could benefit from by eating from the forbidden tree. Eve told God it was the serpent's deception that caused her to violate His Word. Today, many call this, *the power of suggestion.* Nevertheless, it is all evil because it garners vanity.

Vanity is evil because it means devoid of truth and appropriateness, perverseness, depravity, frailty, want of vigor (mental energy, enthusiasm, and determination). It is also emptiness, falsehood, nothingness, emptiness of speech, lying, and worthlessness (of conduct). Vain people are inordinately proud of their appearance, possessions, or achievements. They think and care more for themselves than for anyone else, *even God!* Because they are conceited and have a high, often exaggerated, opinion of themselves or their accomplishments, they are vain.

Eve's heart became full of vanity which enabled the serpent to deceive her. The serpent simply convinced her that she would not die, per God's instructions to Adam. He introduced <u>greed</u> to Eve by convincing her that the fruit would be good to her and it would benefit her. Eve allowed greed to enter her heart because God had already freely given them the pleasure of eating from every tree in the garden except one. "And the LORD God commanded the man, saying, "Of every tree of the garden you may freely eat; but of the tree of the knowledge of good and evil you shall not eat, for in the day that you eat of it you shall surely die" Genesis 2:16-17 (NKJV). When was enough going to be enough for Eve? The serpent played on the vanity within her heart to deceive her. "Then the serpent said to the woman, "<u>*You*</u> will not surely die. For God knows that in the day <u>*you*</u> eat of it *your* eyes will be opened and *you* will be *like God*, knowing good and evil." So when the woman *saw* that the tree was *good for food*, that it was *pleasant to the eyes*, and a tree desirable to *make one wise*, she took of its fruit and ate. She also gave to her husband with her, and he ate" Genesis 3:4-6 (NKJV). You see how the serpent presented everything to be good for Eve. In her deceived mind, all she heard was, "This is good for you, so eat the fruit!" This form of deception occurs a *million times over* in the hearts of God's people everywhere. Satan does not use a club or a gun to threaten humans with so they will be deceived; he simply plants ungodly influences in the heart of god's people to elicit lust. Many fall prey to Satan's suggestive deception because of the vanity that is already in them! Many desire things because they believe their flesh will benefit from them, even if these things violate God's will. If you think you cannot be deceived, you are deceived *already!*

What characteristics did the human heart take on after the fall in the Garden of Eden? The hearts of God's people became calloused (unfeeling; insensitive). It grew dull and was hardened due to the flesh being subjected to vanity. Humankind grew in wickedness and became more self-serving. Jesus explained the reason for His follower's spiritual blindness. He also revealed the reasoning for the lack of understanding, wisdom, knowledge and discernment. He said, "Therefore I speak to them in parables, because seeing they do not see, and hearing they do not hear, nor do they understand. And in them the prophecy of Isaiah is fulfilled, which says: 'Hearing you will hear and shall not understand, and seeing you will see and not perceive; for the hearts of this people have grown dull. Their ears are hard of hearing, and their eyes they have closed, lest they should see with their eyes and hear with their ears, lest they should understand with their hearts and turn, so that I should heal them" Matthew 13:13-15 (NKJV). Spiritual blindness is a term seldom used in the Christian church because false leaders choose not to expose themselves. Nevertheless, God knows and sees these evil workers who will be judged accordingly!

Most Christians truly believe they serve God according to His will. They also believe they are in a ministry which teaches the full counsel of God's Kingdom. The reality is, many churches have been invaded by a multitude of false teachers and preachers! There's a conglomerate of religious leaders who are Satan's ministers of righteousness planted by him in churches throughout the world. The Apostle Paul revealed in 2 Corinthians 11:13-15 (NKJV) – "For such are false apostles, deceitful workers, transforming themselves into apostles of Christ. And no wonder! For Satan himself transforms himself into an angel of light. Therefore it is no great thing if his ministers also transform themselves into ministers of righteousness, whose end will be according to their works." Unfortunately, many parishioners will be blindly led into the dark things of this world!

However, Jesus said in Matthew 15:13-14 (NKJV) – "But He answered and said, "Every plant My heavenly Father has not planted will be uprooted. Let them alone. They are the blind leaders of the blind. And if the blind leads leads the blind, both will fall into a ditch."

Spiritual blindness causes many of our church leaders are preaching and teaching the things that *please the flesh* rather than teaching the Kingdom of God as instructed by Jesus. Many teach things like how to receive a material blessing from the Lord or when a parishioner should receive a harvest. They also teach that the larger the seed offering you give means the larger your harvest or blessings will be! This type teaching stimulates the flesh to desire more and more of the things of this world. This type teaching diametrically opposes God's Word because the Bible promotes God's Spirit and not the flesh. "For if you live according to the *flesh* you will die; but if by the Spirit you put to death the deeds of the body, you will live" Romans 8:13 (NKJV). "So then, those who are in the *flesh* cannot please God" Romans 8:8 (NKJV).

Furthermore, believers must always pray for spiritual wisdom and understanding. Paul, an Apostle of Jesus Christ by the will of God said to the saints who are in Ephesus, "I do not cease to give thanks for you, making mention of you in my prayers: that the God of our Lord Jesus Christ, the Father of glory, may give to you the spirit of wisdom and revelation in the knowledge of Him, *the eyes of your understanding being enlightened*; that you may know what is the hope of His calling, what are the riches of the glory of His inheritance in the saints, and what is the exceeding greatness of His power toward us who believe, according to the working of His mighty power which He worked in Christ when He raised Him from the dead and seated Him at His right hand in the heavenly places" Ephesians 1:16-20 (NKJV).

Teaching those which benefit the flesh redirects believers away from the truth of human suffering. Suffering is a major component of God's curse for the earth and it is for our sake! "Cursed is the ground for your sake; in toil you shall eat of it all the days of your life. Both thorns and thistles it shall bring forth for you" Genesis 3:17-18 (NKJV). As faithful believers, we must enter into the sufferings of Jesus Christ. "Beloved, do not think it strange concerning the fiery trial which is to try you, as though some strange thing happened to you; but rejoice to the extent that you partake of Christ's sufferings, that when His glory is revealed, you may also be glad with exceeding joy" 1 Peter 4:12-13 (NKJV). Human suffering avails believers to present their bodies as living sacrifices, holy, acceptable to God.

Eve was blind to the lust of her flesh and to the serpent's deception. She and Adam were created in God's image, but when God gave them a choice in life, they did not use godly wisdom and became disobedient. Please do not look at Eve as some weak person who should have done better. You would be right if you did, but understand that what happened to Eve happens to millions upon millions of God's people every day! It should not happen because God has given us spiritual weapons to avoid such vanity in our lives. That is, if we surrender to the direction of His Spirit. However, it does show how easily we can be deceived even with the Holy Spirit.

We are sinful creatures (*sinful flesh*) who must be delivered from this bondage of corruption. Please understand we have no obligation to live according to our flesh. "Therefore, brethren, we are debtors—not to the flesh, to live according to the flesh. For if you live according to the flesh you will die; but if by the Spirit you put to death the deeds of the body, you will live. For as many as are led by the Spirit of God, these are sons of God" Romans 8:12-14 (NKJV). Many live only to please the lust of the flesh. We must learn to deny our flesh by the power of the Holy Spirit! Therefore, it is up to the believer not to conform to this world and its appetites.

Believers should clearly understand the nature of their being and those traits that are within them. Once again I repeat Romans 8:20 (KJV) – "For the creature was made subject to vanity, not willingly, but by reason of him who hath subjected the same in hope." Therefore, vanity may be in our DNA, but God has sent us Jesus Christ for deliverance and the power of the Holy Spirit to help us maintain deliverance. We *do not* have to submit to the lustful desires of our flesh! Lustful flesh is of this world, not of born-again Spirit-filled believers. "For all that is in the world—the *lust* of the flesh, the *lust* of the eyes, and the *pride of life*—is not of the Father but is of the world" 1 John 2:16 (NKJV). We have power through God's Spirit to **resist** the devil and the lust of the flesh. This is another situation where believers need to *press* themselves, their heart and mind to respond in obedience to the Lord's will. "And from the days of John the Baptist until now the kingdom of heaven suffers violence and the violent take it by force" Matthew 11:12 (NKJV). *Taking the Kingdom by force* is like someone who possesses eagerness and zeal that press their way into the kingdom, instead of yielding to the opposition of religious foes such as the scribes and Pharisees so as to possess it for their own salvation. The gospel of God's Kingdom enlightens the believer in a sundry of ways to overcome Satan and all of his forces.

Jesus spoke these words to His disciples, "And he said unto them, unto you it is given to know the mystery of the kingdom of God: but unto them that are without, all these things are done in parables" Mark 4:11 (KJV). In other words, only a few individuals like Jesus'; disciples are given to know and understand the mysteries of the kingdom of God. There are reasons that only Jesus' disciples were given to see, hear and understand the mysteries of the Kingdom of heaven. His disciples were not only learners, but they were believers who *surrendered everything* to follow Jesus. They left families, friends, jobs and their livelihoods to follow Jesus. Such commitment and determination meant they were worthy to receive the revelation and insight of the Gospel of the Kingdom.

Disciples and saints abide in God's Word. They are obedient vessels before the Lord who bear good fruit. A saint is described as a most holy thing. Both disciples and saints love one another, bear fruit and imitate their teacher, Jesus Christ. They deny themselves to do the work of God's Kingdom and are able to take up their own cross. "Then Jesus said to His disciples, "If anyone desires to come after Me, let him deny himself, and take up his cross, and follow Me" Matthew 16:24 (NKJV). To deny the self is to forget self, lose sight of self and one's own interests. The cross, which all believers must bear, denotes enduring severe affliction or trials. It also means self-denial. The cross is metaphorically a renunciation of the world that characterizes the true Christian life. It is putting off those things of the flesh with its passions and lusts and live a life of true holiness. Only a few Christians are willing to give themselves to Jesus and to the cause of God's Kingdom this way! "Since you have been raised to new life with Christ, set your sights on the realities of heaven, where Christ sits in the place of honor at God's right hand. Think about the things of heaven, not the things of earth. For you died to this life, and your real life is hidden with Christ in God" Colossians 3:1-3 (NLT).

Jesus said, "If anyone comes to Me and does not hate his father and mother, wife and children, brothers and sisters, yes, and his own life also, he cannot be My disciple. And whoever does not bear his cross and come after Me cannot be My disciple" Luke 14:26-33 (NKJV). So a believer cannot become a disciple without giving up everything they own. Disciples and saints of God give up themselves; therefore, their parents can no longer claim ownership because they were brought with a price. Disciples belong to God! "Or do you not know that your body is the temple of the Holy Spirit who is in you, whom you have from God, and you are not your own? For you were bought at a price; therefore glorify God in your body and in your spirit, which are God's" 1 Corinthians 6:19-20 (NKJV). Neither can anyone say they are in one flesh with their spouse for they belong to Jesus.

The difference between disciples and saints of God versus other Christians is they fulfill God's calling in their lives. They are faithful, trustworthy and obedient! The Lord has that one thing that is more important than anything else, He has their hearts! Jesus said to him, "You shall love the LORD your God with all your heart, with all your soul, and with all your mind" Matthew 22:37 (NKJV). Many Christian believers say they love the Lord and are willing to follow Him according to all the requirements of the cross, but that is all they do, talk! They may desire to, but the fulfillment is not there! This is similar to Jesus parable of the two sons.

"But what do you think? A man had two sons, and he came to the first and said, 'Son, go, work today in my vineyard.' He answered and said, 'I will not,' but afterward he regretted it and went. Then he came to the second and said likewise. And he answered and said, 'I go, sir,' but he did not go. Which of the two did the will of his father?" They said to Him, "The first." Jesus said to them, "Assuredly, I say to you that tax collectors and harlots enter the kingdom of God before you. For John came to you in the way of righteousness,

and you did not believe him; but tax collectors and harlots believed him; and when you saw it, you did not afterward relent and believe him" Matthew *21:28-32 (NKJV).*

Many Christians are like the second son who said, 'I go, sir,' but he did not go. Hence, whatever they do not have, even what they have will be taken away from him. Spiritually speaking, seeing they do not see, and hearing they do not hear, nor do they understand. These individuals consume themselves with other things in life: Things that please their flesh!

At best, Christians equally *share* their time with the Lord and all of their other life affairs. The Lord should come first before anyone else. This is the price for being His disciple. "A large crowd was following Jesus. He turned around and said to them, "If you want to be my disciple, you must hate everyone else by comparison—your father and mother, wife and children, brothers and sisters—yes, even your own life. Otherwise, you cannot be my disciple" Luke 14:25-26 (NLT). Many believers like to share their love for Jesus with their families, occupations, entertainment, hobbies and specific gifts and talents like ministry and/or leaders of an organization. These things can become idols that separate us from God! And believe me, they do become idols. Ministers of God's Word, pastors, evangelists, etc. have the greatest challenge of all because it is easy to become wrapped-up in the glory, popularity, control and wealth of a ministry and make God second in life. There are a lot of God's servants who become vain and selfish due to the honor of their ministerial positions. Because church people esteem these individuals so highly; many become full of themselves. Thus, they desire things from their own hearts versus the things they hear from the Spirit! They become full of greed, control, selfishness, covetous, possessive, lustful and more! Sometimes these desires cause conflicts in a ministry because the parishioners are not in agreement with the leader. When things like this occur, the ministry itself has become the idol and the Lord has become a secondary, *silent* partner.

Idols are images representing false gods. They are gods, other than Jehovah God, to which divine honor is paid. Shamefully, Christians make their local pastors idols as mentioned above. Their affections are strongly (often excessively) set on those above them in ministry. Many a pastor becomes the objects of a passionate devotion--a person's love and adoration. However, a break-through can be made in life when the believer falls passionately in love with Jesus (the true Savior) and lives to worship, meditate, esteem, honor, glorify and commune with Him daily. This event occurs when Jesus become first in their lives The way believers get to this level is to crave or *hunger* and *desire* the Lord with all their heart. It occurs when the believer presses through all the circumstances and glamour of life to follow the Lord. At this level of commitment to Jesus, there is nothing but ultimate *joy and peace*.

By *not* becoming a disciple, few Christians experience this level of joy and peace. Subsequently, they do not hear those things which the Holy Spirit is saying to the church. Nor do they see or understand the Word of the Kingdom. Jesus explains the reasons why this occurs in His parable of the Sower. Few people would believe the level of spiritual blindness that occurs in the church. Apostles Matthew, Mark and Luke recorded this statement: *"He who has ears to hear, let him hear!"* Jesus made this statement several times in referring to the mysteries of the Kingdom. Additionally, at the end of every letter, Jesus wrote to the seven churches in Asia making a similar statement. Jesus said, *"He who has an ear, let him hear what the Spirit says to the churches"* Revelation 2:7 (NKJV). The letters explain in detail the failures and/or shortcomings of the church. The letters were directed to the churches in Asia but the message itself is to *all churches* of the world. Therefore, if you are unable to see, hear and understand according to God's Spirit, you should examine your own ways and motives.

Only A *Few* See and Understand the Truths that Jesus Revealed in His Parables!

Because of spiritual blindness, many in the household of faith are unable to hear, see or understand the insight Jesus gives in these parables. In His teachings, Jesus utters things kept secret from the foundation of the world. "All these things Jesus spoke to the multitude in parables; and without a parable He did not speak to them, that it might be fulfilled which was spoken by the prophet, saying: "I will open My mouth in parables; I will utter things kept secret from the foundation of the world" Matthew 13:34-35 (NKJV). These parables serve not only as spiritual insight to the Jews, but they were also prophesies for future generations. History does repeat itself because we see the same things occurring in today's churches that occurred with the scribes and Pharisees with whom Jesus had conflict. Some of today's Christians are mirroring the rejection of Jesus and the Word of God the same as the Jewish nation. Today's ministries reject the Word of the Kingdom by not teaching the fullness of it! Many prefer to teach events from the Old Testament which do not bear the saving grace of Jesus Christ nor the power of God's Spirit. Therefore, Jesus' parables are extremely important to today's Christians for direction, teachings, prophecy, warnings, making disciples and understanding God's will on earth!

We see the importance of these mysteries (parables) and the Word of God's Kingdom because they are the principles Jesus taught while on earth. The Apostle Paul understood the mysteries and was called to make known the riches of God's glory among the Gentiles. He said, "I now rejoice in my sufferings for you, and fill up in my flesh what is lacking in the afflictions of Christ, for the sake of His body, which is the church, of which I became a minister according to the stewardship from God which was given to me for you, to fulfill the word of God, the mystery which has been hidden from ages and from generations, but now has been revealed to His saints. To them God willed to make known what are the riches of the glory of this mystery among the Gentiles: which is Christ in you, the hope of glory. Him we preach, warning every man and teaching every man in all wisdom, that we may present every man perfect in Christ Jesus. To this end I also labor, striving according to His working which works in me mightily" Colossians 1:24-29 (NKJV).

Not all Christians can see, hear or understand these parables (mysteries). In reality, many of those called by God to minister have difficulty understanding the parables because of their own characteristics and life styles. Jesus parables *conceals truth from those who are either too lazy to think or too blinded by prejudice to see.* The purpose of a parable has always been to illustrate a truth. In life's teachings, when a person cannot see or understand a spiritual situation or matter, a teacher will use a story to help explain the situation. They take something that is familiar to individual(s), something that they can understand and allow them to tell the story. In the story, they illustrate the truth they are trying to get across to them. However, the parables have deeper meanings than ordinary stories. Therefore, the revelation and understanding of these hidden truths only comes to those who are Spirit-filled and live according to God's commandments!

If a believer _truly_ hears the Word of the Kingdom, God's Word will cause a change in that person's perspective, understanding, demeanor and convictions. The reason is the Word of God is living and powerful. It operates on the believer's heart and it penetrates deeply between the soul and the spirit so the individual correctly understands God's Word. It exposes the innermost thoughts and desires of the believer in contrast to God's Word, so the individual will know when he/she has violated God's Word. "For the word of God is living and powerful, and sharper than any two-edged sword, piercing even to the division of soul and spirit, and of joints and marrow, and is a discerner of the thoughts and intents of the heart" Hebrews 4:12 (NKJV).

CHAPTER 3

The Hearts of God's People have Grown Futile!

Jesus Prophesies Spiritual Blindness and Satanic Mixture in the Body of Christ (the Church)!

Jesus wrote seven letters to the angels of the churches in Asia. At the close of each letter, He wrote these words, "He who has an ear, let him hear what the Spirit says to the churches" Revelation 2:7 (NKJV). Jesus made the same identical statement in each letter because the statement is the most pertinent issue facing the church and God's people. In the seven letters, Jesus revealed the short-comings of each ministry and His displeasure with five of them. Most of the churches had experienced significant demonic involvement like He prophesied in the parable of the wheat and the tares. Jesus' teachings and prophesies were always directed to God's people, partially to the church (the body of Christ). A lot of Christians believe Jesus' parables are directed to the world, to give some understanding of the principles of the body of Christ (the church). However, this is not the case. His parables are directed to those in the household of faith. In fact, the Bible itself is directed to God's elect, those He predestined before the world was formed.

God's Word is designed to give clarification to those He calls. It identifies the many issues confronting God's people, their shortcomings, the deception of Satan and his wiles, as well as, the persecution and suffering that all of His people will encounter on the earth! Because the creation was subject to vanity/futility and needed to be delivered from the bondage of corruption *(Romans 8: 20-21)*, a great portion of God's people have missed this mark because of spiritual blindness. This means that many are unable to see, hear or understand the Word of God's Kingdom which reveals the truth of their existence and their ungodly behavior while on the earth. As revealed earlier, <u>vanity</u> means to be devoid of truth and appropriateness, depravity, perverseness, frailty, want of vigor. To understand the significant of this Scripture and its meaning, see the following definitions below:

- *Devoid of truth* – It is completely lacking; destitute or empty and being without <u>truth</u>.
- *Appropriateness* – It is appropriate conduct; doing the right thing and to take for one's own use, especially illegally or without permission.
- *Depravity* – This is behavior that is immoral or evil. It is also moral corruption or degradation.
- *Perverseness* – The perverted is deliberately deviating from what is regarded as normal, good, or proper, deliberate unruliness.
- *Frailty* – This is a fault, especially a moral weakness. It is the condition of having a weak character or weak moral standards.
- *Want of vigor* – This is want of exuberant and resilient strength of body or mind; vitality. It is also active strength or force of body or mind; or capacity for exertion, physically, intellectually, or morally; including force or energy. It means emptiness, falsehood, nothingness, emptiness of speech, lying, and worthlessness (of conduct).

A vain person is inordinately proud of his/her appearance, possessions, or achievements. Knowing that humanity was subject to vanity/futility, we can understand more clearly the reason why all creation, even God's elect, exemplify greed, pride, selfishness, sexual immorality, impurity, lustful pleasures, idolatry, sorcery, hostility, quarreling, jealousy, outbursts of anger, selfish ambition, dissension, division, envy and drunkenness. It is unfortunate that many of these wicked behaviors are saturated deep in the hearts of those who call themselves Christians. These behaviors are also relevant in those called by the Lord to minister truth to God's people.

Here is the problem: As Christians many of us do not recognize that we live according to these behaviors because *only a few* of us have examined our own hearts to see who we really are! Hence, the reason some people are spiritually blind!

Jesus made the probing statement which says, "He who has an ear, let him hear" because a multitude of believers are spiritually blind and cannot "see nor hear" the Word of God's Kingdom. In the *parable of the sower*, Jesus said the reason was due to the dullness of their heart. "And in them the prophecy of Isaiah is fulfilled, which says: 'Hearing you will hear and shall not understand, and seeing you will see and not perceive; for the hearts of this people have grown dull" Matthew 13:14-15 (NKJV). I believe this is especially true for those He called to minister to His people. The dull hearts of God's people resulted from the vanity/futility all creation was subjected to as the result of the fall of man. Here is another major problem! God's people continue to live their daily lives never realizing the breadth and depth of their blindness, thus never seeking deliverance from bondage. The blindness is perpetuated because of false teaching, Satan's deception and their own flesh. When Jesus taught the *parable of the sower* to His followers, He said, "He who has ears to hear, let him hear" Matthew 13:9 (NKJV)! It meant, those who could hear by God's Spirit, let him hear and receive the insight and revelation of what the Spirit is saying! Because so many in the household of faith are spiritually blind, few neither understand the truth of God's Word nor deliver its inherent truths.

Jesus spoke several parables to His followers, which not only revealed why He spoke in parables, but also the reason God's people did not hear, see nor understand the Word of the Kingdom. Jesus' parables gave further explanation of how God's people are deceived by Satan and the reason a mixture of good and evil occurs in the church as result of false preaching and teaching. He also gave understanding of those who give their lives to the Kingdom and who will be saved, and attend the wedding supper (Matthew 22:1-14).

The parable of the wheat and tares is significant to the body of Christ (the church). It reveals how Satan was able to plant his *ministers of unrighteousness* and *evil workers* in church. The parable reveals how the Lord allows both wicked ministers and parishioners to remain in the church, until the end of the age.

The Parable of the Wheat and the Tares
"Another parable He put forth to them, saying: "The kingdom of heaven is like a man who sowed good seed in his field; but while men slept, his enemy came and sowed tares among the wheat and went his way. But when the grain had sprouted and produced a crop, then the tares also appeared. So the servants of the owner came and said to him, 'Sir, did you not sow good seed in your field? How then does it have tares?' He said to them, 'An enemy has done this.' The servants said to him, 'Do you want us then to go and gather them up?' But he said, 'No, lest while you gather up the tares you also uproot the wheat with them. Let both grow together until the harvest, and at the time of harvest I will say to the reapers, "First gather together the tares and bind them in bundles to burn them, but gather the wheat into my barn" Matthew 13:24-30 (NKJV).

The Parable of the Tares Explained
"Then Jesus sent the multitude away and went into the house. And His disciples came to Him, saying, "Explain to us the parable of the tares of the field." He answered and said to them: "He who sows the good seed is the Son of Man. The field is the world, the good seeds are the sons of the kingdom, but the tares are the sons of the wicked one. The enemy who sowed them is the devil, the harvest is the end of the age, and the reapers are the angels.

Therefore as the tares are gathered and burned in the fire, so it will be at the end of this age. The Son of Man will send out His angels, and they will gather out of His kingdom all things that offend, and those who practice lawlessness, and will cast them into the furnace of fire. There will be wailing and gnashing of teeth. Then the righteous will shine forth as the sun in the kingdom of their Father. He who has ears to hear, let him hear" Matthew 13:36-43 (NKJV)!

The parable of the wheat and tares depicts the *spiritual blindness* of God's people on the earth. This parable is extremely insightful to the body of

Christ because it reveals Satan's influence in the lives of ordinary church people. Jesus gave the meaning of this parable to His disciples as revealed in Scripture. However, there is even greater insight and a deeper revelation revealed by the Holy Spirit! It is illuminated only to Spirit-filled believers who have ears to hear what the Spirit is saying to the church! Please carefully read and discern this insight in the following paragraph. This parable reveals the reason for false teaching and the proliferation of evil workers in today's churches! It also reveals how a multitude of Christians are seeking after messages that satisfy their flesh instead of those challenging the soul to becoming more holy and righteous before the Lord.

- *The kingdom of heaven is like a man who sowed good seed in his field; but while men slept, his enemy came and sowed tares among the wheat and went his way* – The kingdom is described many different ways but it is still God's Kingdom: It is written in The Word as the Kingdom of heaven, the Kingdom of God, Jesus' Kingdom and the Kingdom which are all the same. The Kingdom can be entered on earth and/or inherited hereafter. It is the royal power, kingship, dominion and rule of Jesus Christ in the hearts of those who believe in Him and have submitted their will to Him. The Kingdom falls into two classes.

   The first class is viewed as present and involves suffering for those who enter it. "Which is manifest evidence of the righteous judgment of God that you may be counted worthy of the kingdom of God, for which you also suffer" 2 Thessalonians 1:5 (NKJV). The second class is viewed as in the future and is associated with reward and glory. "Then the King will say to those on His right hand, 'Come, you blessed of My Father, inherit the kingdom prepared for you from the foundation of the world" Matthew 25:34 (NKJV). Please understand that the Kingdom of God is within you, it is in your heart! "Now when He was asked by the Pharisees when the kingdom of God would come, He answered them and said, "The kingdom of God does not come with observation; nor will they say, 'See here!' or 'See there!' For indeed, the kingdom of God is within you" Luke 17:20-21 (NKJV). Therefore, wherever Jesus Christ is and wherever His rule is demonstrated, this is the Kingdom! He is foremost in the heart of the believer and substantiated in His churches through the very lives of Believers who are faithful and obedient.

- As stated by Jesus, "He who sows the good seed is the Son of Man *(Jesus)*. The field is the world *(God's creation)*, the good seeds are the sons *(daughters too)* of the kingdom, but the tares are the sons *(daughters too)* of the wicked one *(Satan)*. The term, *while men slept* is a spiritual dynamic that demonstrates how those who took on the spirit of vanity became slaves to the bondage of corruption. To sleep means to yield to sloth and sin and to be indifferent to one's salvation. The essence of sleeping is the ungodly and wicked corruption that occurs in the people of God, both Jews and Christians. It is when Satan's demons are allowed to *sow tares with the wheat*. Tares are known as degenerate wheat. Their seeds are poisonous to man and herbivorous animals, producing sleepiness, nausea, convulsions and even death. Symbolically, this is what happens in the Christian church when men and women who are influenced by Satan even as members of a local assembly. These individuals are like placing bad apples in a bunch of good ones.

  Therefore, yielding to sloth and sin occurs in God's people when they neglect the truth of the Word and began to obey the commandments of men. Satan and his deacons have been able to influence many of God's people to process vanity and seek those things which satisfy their flesh. These individuals have a form of godliness but they deny the power of God's Spirit! They should be fearful of the Lord by the way they think, scheme and attempt to satisfy their flesh through greed, sexual exploitation, selfishness, vanity and the like.

  o <u>Tares are Christians that Turn-away From Sound Doctrine to Fables!</u> - Tares are individuals who worship God in vain! They turn away from the truth of God's Word to fables.

Tares are both Christian parishioners, as well as, Christian leaders (Apostles, prophets, pastors, evangelists and teachers). These are normal people that have been influenced by Satan to become selfish, vain and ungodly in their thoughts. They consider themselves servants of righteousness, but are greatly deceived! Some of them become flamboyant speakers who lure parishioners with promises from God of wealth, a harvest and/or substantial blessings that are always coming but never seem to arrive! Paul spoke of these individuals to the church at Corinth. He said, "But I will continue doing what I have always done. This will undercut those who are looking for an opportunity to boast that their work is just like ours. These people are false apostles. They are deceitful workers who disguise themselves as apostles of Christ. But I am not surprised! Even Satan disguises himself as an angel of light. So it is no wonder that his servants also disguise themselves as servants of righteousness. In the end they will get the punishment their wicked deeds deserve" 2 Corinthians 11:12-15 (NLT).

Jesus' apostles also spoke of the dynamics of these unholy, deceptive leaders. Their words constantly warned us that many false prophets, teachers and ministers of the Gospel would become great in God's house in the last days. Well… here we are… in the last days and a multitude of these individuals have planted themselves among the Christian church.

It is amazing how history repeats itself over and over again. We seem to re-live the same set of ungodly circumstances and never grow and develop in the things of the Lord. Before the false prophets and teachers of today, there were the scribes and the Pharisees of yesterday. Both rejected the truth of God's Word and Jesus Christ. They just did it in different ways. The scribes went beyond interpretation of Scripture, however, and added many man-made traditions to what God had said. Jesus called-out both the scribes and the Pharisees regarding their traditions and wayward ways, as seen below:

"What sorrow awaits you teachers of religious law and you Pharisees. Hypocrites! For you cross land and sea to make one convert, and then you turn that person into twice the child of hell you yourselves are!

"Blind guides! What sorrow awaits you! For you say that it means nothing to swear 'by God's Temple,' but that it is binding to swear 'by the gold in the Temple.' Blind fools! Which is more important—the gold or the Temple that makes the gold sacred? And you say that to swear 'by the altar' is not binding, but to swear 'by the gifts on the altar' is binding. How blind! For which is more important—the gift on the altar or the altar that makes the gift sacred? When you swear 'by the altar,' you are swearing by it and by everything on it. And when you swear 'by the Temple,' you are swearing by it and by God, who lives in it. And when you swear 'by heaven,' you are swearing by the throne of God and by God, who sits on the throne.

"What sorrow awaits you teachers of religious law and you Pharisees? Hypocrites! For you are careful to tithe even the tiniest income from your herb gardens, but you ignore the more important aspects of the law—justice, mercy, and faith. You should tithe, yes, but do not neglect the more important things. Blind guides! You strain your water so you won't accidentally swallow a gnat, but you swallow a camel!

"What sorrow awaits you teachers of religious law and you Pharisees? Hypocrites! For you are so careful to clean the outside of the cup and the dish, but inside you are filthy—full of greed and self-indulgence! You blind Pharisee! First wash the inside of the cup and the dish, and then the outside will become clean, too.

"What sorrow awaits you teachers of religious law and you Pharisees? Hypocrites! For you are like whitewashed tombs—beautiful on the outside but filled on the inside with dead people's bones and all sorts of impurity. Outwardly you look like righteous people, but inwardly your hearts are filled with hypocrisy and lawlessness.

"What sorrow awaits you teachers of religious law and you Pharisees? Hypocrites! For you build tombs for the prophets your ancestors killed, and you decorate the monuments of the godly people your ancestors destroyed. Then you say, 'If we had lived in the days of our ancestors, we would never have joined them in killing the prophets.'

But in saying that, you testify against yourselves that you are indeed the descendants of those who murdered the prophets. Go ahead and finish what your ancestors started. Snakes! Sons of vipers! How will you escape the judgment of hell" Matthew 23:15-33 (NLT)?

Today's false teachers are like unthinking animals, creatures of instinct, born to be caught and destroyed. They scoff at things they do not understand and teach things that tickle the ears of parishioners for high financial rewards! Their destruction is their reward for the harm they have done. They love to indulge in evil pleasures and they delight in deception. They commit adultery with both their eyes and with their bodies. They are just like the Pharisees and worship the Lord in lip service only. Jesus said, "Hypocrites! Well did Isaiah prophesy about you, saying: 'These people draw near to Me with their mouth, and honor Me with their lips, but their heart is far from Me. And in vain they worship Me, teaching as doctrines *the commandments of men*" Matthew 15:7-9 (NKJV)

Unfortunately, only a small number of believers have spiritual eyes to see the deception which emanates from these individuals. It seems that the church world has completely ignored the writings of Jesus, the apostle Paul and the other apostles where they fore-warn us of the tares that would infect the church. Here's a list of are some of their warnings:

Matthew warned us - *"And Jesus answered and said to them: "Take heed that no one deceives you. For many will come in My name, saying, 'I am the Christ,' and will deceive many" Matthew 24:4-5 (NKJV).*

Paul warned us - *"Preach the word! Be ready in season and out of season. Convince, rebuke, exhort, with all longsuffering and teaching. For the time will come when they will not endure sound doctrine, but according to their own desires, because they have itching ears, they will heap up for themselves teachers; and they will turn their ears away from the truth, and be turned aside to fables" 2 Timothy 4:2-4 (NKJV).*

Titus warned us - *"For there are many insubordinate, both idle talkers and deceivers, especially those of the circumcision, whose mouths must be stopped, who subvert whole households, teaching things which they ought not, for the sake of dishonest gain. One of them, a prophet of their own, said, "Cretans are always liars, evil beasts, and lazy gluttons." This testimony is true. Therefore rebuke them sharply, that they may be sound in the faith, not giving heed to Jewish fables and commandments of men who turn from the truth. To the pure all things are pure, but to those who are defiled and unbelieving nothing is pure; but even their mind and conscience are defiled. They profess to know God, but in works they deny Him, being abominable, disobedient, and disqualified for every good work" Titus 1:10-16 (NKJV).*

Peter warned us – *"But there were also false prophets among the people, even as there will be false teachers among you, who will secretly bring in destructive heresies, even denying the Lord who bought them, and bring on themselves swift destruction. And many will follow their destructive ways, because of whom the way of truth will be blasphemed. By covetousness they will exploit you with deceptive words; for a long time their judgment has not been idle, and their destruction does not slumber" 2 Peter 2:1-3 (NKJV).*

Jude warned us – *"But you, beloved, remember the words which were spoken before by the apostles of our Lord Jesus Christ: how they told you that there would be mockers in the last time who would walk according to their own ungodly lusts. These are sensual persons, who cause divisions, not having the Spirit" Jude 1:17-19 (NKJV).*

As you can see, several apostles identified the emergence of false prophets, teachers and spiritual leaders that would rise up and *deceive many*. They spoke to the false teachers and leaders of their day, as well as prophesied the emergence of false teachers and leaders in our day. We know Satan has planted tares in the body of Christ, for we see daily evidence of that. These individuals are bringing death to the church and to good people who are following them. It is not a matter of *will there* be false preaching and false teaching; it is already a common place within the borders our churches. This greater question is will any of God's people generate sufficient insight and godly wisdom to overcome this obstacle? Jude gave us some good advice regarding the presence of these ungodly individuals. He said, "But you, dear friends, must build each other up in your most holy faith, pray in the power of the Holy Spirit, and await the mercy of our Lord Jesus Christ, who will bring you eternal life. In this way, you will keep yourselves safe in God's love. And you must show mercy to those whose faith is wavering. Rescue others by snatching them from the flames of judgment. Show mercy to still others, but do so with great caution, hating the sins that contaminate their lives" Jude 1:20-23 (NLT).

"He who sows the good seed is the Son of Man. The field is the world, the good seeds are the sons of the kingdom, but the tares are the sons of the wicked one. The enemy who sowed them is the devil, the harvest is the end of the age, and the reapers are the angels" Matthew13:37-39 (NKJV) – Now, we know that Jesus is the Son of Man. The field is the world; God's creation and the good seeds are those who love Jesus and are faithful to Him. More importantly, the good seed are the ones who are *obedient* to the Lord and to God's Word. A lot of Christians like to replace the word *obedience* with *grace*. Grace does have an important role in the Kingdom of God. It is rendered by the Lord at Divine times and for a Divine purpose. However, do not buy-in to the concept that God's grace will override disobedience. Please do not be deceived and become a tare yourself!

Satan, our enemy, continues to influence and deceive men and women of God in order to take their birthright of eternal salvation. We are in the last days so our time is limited. We must get this thing right now! The tares and the wheat will continue to grow and live together until the end of time. God's angels will do the separating at the end of the age and at that time *it will be too late* to change your mind. I hope and pray that you will receive your reward and not be as those spoken of in the parable of the ten virgins, who did not make it. "Afterward the other virgins came also, saying, 'Lord, Lord, open to us!' But he answered and said, 'Assuredly, I say to you, I do not know you.' "Watch therefore, for you know neither the day nor the hour in which the Son of Man is coming" Matthew 25:11-13 (NKJV).

Now is the time for you to rise up and prepare the way of the Lord! Many say they desire to be saved, but only a few seem willing to press forward to achieve it! You can no longer look to the right or the left for help because your help will come from the Lord. That is, *after you* seek His will and authority in your life.

We can talk about all those things that happen to God's people, the Jewish nation, but that will not help any of us to be saved. We can also blame false teachers and ministers for the deceit and the deception in the church. We would be correct, but that will not help us to be saved either. There will be only one person answering to the Lord on judgment day and that person is *you!* You make it right now or find out how wrong you were on judgment day! God has given us everything we need to be graded righteous and worthy on the day we stand before His throne. We have an advocate in Jesus Christ who supports us in all the things we do, if our hearts are right. However, we are the ones who must use the weapons God has given to battle the evil forces in this world.

FACTORS THAT CAUSE CHRISTIANS BLINDNESS!
Spiritual blindness is a serious matter that plagues the body of Christ! The parable of the wheat and the tares reveals the mixture that causes false teaching and spiritual blindness. Regrettably, not many ministers teach the influx of spiritual blindness and what to do about it. Therefore, the people of God are left unaware of this serious problem! Most parishioners believe today's ministers are equipping them to do God's work in the body of Christ. They sincerely believe they are being matured in the Lord, measuring up to the full and complete standard of Christ. Yet, the church's witness in the world does not reflect this perceived growth and maturity! This is the reality that God's people need to understand and change. Many factors are driving this paradigm such as Satan's deception, false teaching, the lust of human flesh and Christians refusing to seek sound doctrine. They are choosing to follow their own desires and will look for teachers who will tell them whatever their itching ears want to hear. On top of all of this, many are spiritually blind. I realize, of course, no one thinks they are spiritually blind; just like many Christians, they believe they are going to be saved. Satan's deception in the church has caused this issue. This is the reason we need to look at the parable of the wheat and the tares with spiritual eyes and ears to discern what God's Spirit is telling us! Here is my summary:

Jesus revealed the magnitude of the enemy's deception in this parable. The parable is explained as such, "Another parable He put forth to them, saying: "The kingdom of heaven is like a man who sowed good seed in his field; but while men slept, his enemy came and sowed tares among the wheat and went his way. But when the grain had sprouted and produced a crop, then the tares also appeared. So the servants of the owner came and said to him, 'Sir, did you not sow good seed in your field? How then does it have tares?' He said to them, 'An enemy has done this" Matthew 13:24-28 (NKJV). Jesus gave clarity to the individuals involved in this prophecy. "He answered and said to them: "He who sows the good seed is the Son of Man. The field is the world, the good seeds are the sons of the kingdom, but the tares are the sons of the wicked one. The enemy who sowed them is the devil, the harvest is the end of the age, and the reapers are the angels" Matthew 13:37-39 (NKJV). Once again, I give the meaning to this parable so all believers will understand completely what is happening in the house of God.

Jesus said that the Kingdom *is like* a man who sowed good seed in his field. In other words, the Kingdom, which is the royal power and dignity conferred on Christians in the Messiah's kingdom, is the good seed in the church. We know Jesus said the field is the world, so it is the church's responsibility to sow good seed in the world through the ministry of those called by the Lord to teach the Word of God. This word develops and matures worthy saints as a witness to the world. So the church *is like* a man who sowed good seed in his field. As mention, the good seed are the sons of the kingdom. The sons of the Kingdom are Christian believers *(saints of God)* who live according to God's Spirit and not their flesh. "For as many as are led by the Spirit of God, these are sons of God" Romans 8:14 (NKJV). Please understand what Jesus is saying. He is revealing that He, Jesus Christ, sowed good seed (good Christians) in His church.

And He (Jesus) Himself gave some to be apostles, some prophets, some evangelists, and some pastors and teachers, for the equipping of the saints for the work of ministry, for the edifying of the body of Christ, till we all come to the unity of the faith and of the knowledge of the Son of God, to a perfect man, to the measure of the stature of the fullness of Christ; that we should no longer be children, tossed to and fro and carried about with every wind of

doctrine, by the trickery of men, in the cunning craftiness of deceitful plot-
ting, but, speaking the truth in love, may grow up in all things into Him who
is the head—Christ—from whom the whole body, joined and knit together by
what every joint supplies, according to the effective working by which every
part does its share, causes growth of the body for the edifying of itself in love"
Ephesians 4:11-16 (NKJV).

The aforementioned Scriptures describe how Jesus sows good seed in His
field. It is done through anointed men and women called by the Lord to
edify the body of Christ till we all come to the unity of the faith and of
the knowledge of the Son of God, to a perfect man, to the measure of the
stature of the fullness of Christ. But while men slept, his enemy came and
sowed tares among the wheat and went his way. Jesus is revealing that
He had good Christian people in His church, but while they (the body of
Christ–Christian leaders and parishioners) slept, Satan came and sowed
tares through deception. Sleep means to yield to sloth and sin and to be
indifferent to one's salvation. This is the result of God's curse. Remember,
the curse subjected God's creation to vanity and futility. God's people
have been sleep for a number of untold years Even Jesus disciples slept.
"Then He came to the disciples and found them sleeping, and said to
Peter, "What! Could you not watch with Me one hour? Watch and pray,
lest you enter into temptation. The spirit indeed is willing, but the flesh is
weak" Matthew 26:40-41 (NKJV). The church's sleeping is validated in
the parable of the ten virgins. The ten virgins are figuratively of a local
church in its relation to Christ. Matthew 25:5 (NKJV) reveals, "But while
the bridegroom was delayed, they (the virgins) all slumbered and slept."

According to Jesus, the tares are the sons of the wicked one. These
are wicked individuals that have been planted by Satan in the church. As
mentioned earlier, they serve as pastors, teachers, evangelists, choir members, intercessors, deacons and the like. Paul spoke of these individuals in
2 Corinthians 11:12-15 (NKJV) – "But what I do, I will also continue to
do, that I may cut off the opportunity from those who desire an opportunity to be regarded just as we are in the things of which they boast. For
such are false apostles, deceitful workers, transforming themselves into

apostles of Christ. And no wonder! For Satan himself transforms himself into an angel of light. Therefore it is no great thing if his ministers also transform themselves into ministers of righteousness, whose end will be according to their works."

These individuals were at one time well-meaning Christians who desired to advance the Kingdom of God. Just like Eve, they were influenced by Satan to fulfill the desires of the flesh. Because Satan is cunning and deceptive, he is able to persuade many to take on different evil spirits such as greed, vanity, control, selfishness, idolatry and more! He constantly shows God's people how some things, those which violate God's Word, will be good for them! And like he did to Eve, he said, "*You* will not die, *your* eyes will be opened, *you* will be like God and *you* will know good and evil." It is you, you, you! He gets the individual to lust after the things that will benefit him or her! Many wayward ministers have learned this technique because the flesh seeks after material blessings from the Lord.

Many say, "Your blessing is on the way, you will receive a harvest when you plant seeds in the ministry or you are the head and not the tail so God will reward you." One of the *most used* money raising ploys is the Scriptures are found in Luke 6:38 (NKJV) – "Give and it will be given to you: good measure, pressed down, shaken together, and running over will be put into your bosom." The Scripture has been *misused* over and over again; however, in this passage the Lord is not referring to money at all! He is referring to our ability to live a Kingdom life. The Scripture advises us how to live a kingdom life by forgiving and loving, not condemning nor judging. The last part of the Scripture reads, "For with the same measure that you use, it will be measured back to you" Luke 6:38 (NKJV). The revelation of the Scripture is this: The measures you use to love, forgive, judge and condemn others in your life is the *same measures* God will use to love, forgive, judge and condemn you! So, from what do you seek deliverance, the bondage of corruption or material blessings? Enough said? James said, "You ask and do not receive, because you ask amiss, that you may spend it on your pleasures" James 4:3 (NKJV).

No one likes to admit it but our churches are full of these grievous individuals. They talk more about money and planting a seed than they do the Gospel of the Kingdom. In fact, these ministers have not been given the insight of the Kingdom, because they, too, are spiritually blind. The Apostle Peter reveals their character when he said, "But there were also false prophets among the people, even as there will be false teachers among you, who will secretly bring in destructive heresies, even denying the Lord who bought them, and bring on themselves swift destruction. And many will follow their destructive ways, because of whom the way of truth will be blasphemed. By covetousness they will exploit you with deceptive words; for a long time their judgment has not been idle, and their destruction does not slumber" 2 Peter 2:1-3 (NKJV).

Because our time on the earth is short, believers everywhere must press forward in their *hearts* to God's Kingdom. You may have to do your own studying and ask the Lord for insight to God's Word because some Christian ministries do not teach the full counsel of God's Word. Furthermore, while seeking the truth of God's Word, you must keep your heart *pure* and do not *quench* the Holy Spirit by engaging in wickedness. Just know that only those who live according to God's Spirit will know the truth of the Word of God's Kingdom, as well as enter, or inherit it. "For what the law could not do in that it was weak through the flesh, God did by sending His own Son in the likeness of sinful flesh, on account of sin: He condemned sin in the flesh, that the righteous requirement of the law might be fulfilled in us who *do not walk* according to the flesh but according to the Spirit" Romans 8:3-4 (NKJV). The parable of the ten virgins validates this truth and reveals that only Spirit-filled believers enter the Lord's wedding feast.

In the parable of the sower, Jesus gives insight as to why only Spirit-filled believers understand the Word of the Kingdom. Jesus said, "*When anyone hears the word of the kingdom, and does not understand it*, then the wicked one comes and snatches away what was sown in his heart. This is he who received seed by the wayside" Matthew 13:19 (NKJV). Have you ever thought about how many individuals attend church; hear the truth of the Gospel; and yet still do not understand the Word of God's Kingdom? It is because they are still under the influence of Satan; for he snatches away any truth that was sown in their heart. The routine of going to church and hearing God's Word while not understanding it, continues to be lived out in born-again believers. However, they have quenched God's Spirit because of their wicked behaviors.

Jesus also said, "But he who received the seed on stony places, this is he who hears the word and immediately receives it with joy; yet he has no root in himself, but endures only for a while. For when tribulation or persecution arises because of the word, immediately he stumbles" Matthew 13:20-21 (NKJV). As believers of Jesus Christ, we are ordained to enter the same suffering as Jesus did. "For to this you were called, because Christ also suffered for us, leaving us an example, that you should follow His steps" 1 Peter 2:21 (NKJV). Throughout our lives on earth, God's people will suffer hardships, troubles, needs, loss, afflictions, persecutions and much more! Therefore, as tribulations and/or persecutions continue to rise, many Christians will stumble by not knowing the truth of God's Word. The word _stumble_ has many meanings in this Scripture. It means to be offended, to entice to sin, to fall away, to cause one to judge unfavorably or unjustly of another, to be displeasured at a thing and to make indignant. As mentioned before, there are many individuals who attend church, hear the Word of God's Kingdom and yet because of tribulation, persecution or spiritual blindness, they fail to grow or mature.

Jesus revealed another cause of spiritual blindness. He said, "*Now he who received seed among the thorns* is he who hears the word, and the cares of this world and the deceitfulness of riches choke the word, and he becomes unfruitful" Matthew 13:22 (NKJV). There are others who receive the Word of the Kingdom among the thorns. Thorns represent trials, tribulations, tests, afflictions, hardships, chastisements, sorrows and sufferings in our lives. When an individual experiences these tribulations and hears God's Word, the cares of this world and the deceitfulness of riches chokes the word. The message is crowded out by the worries of life and the lure of wealth and no fruit is produced. Many of the Lord's servants (ministers) become unfruitful because of the deceitfulness of riches. They may start out strong and faithful in ministry, but they are soon caught-up in the cares of this life. They began to lust and greed for money, control and power in the ministry. Thus, these individuals become vain, selfish and out-of-control. Because they do not teach the truth of God's Word, but the minister fables to support their theology, many of their converts are not only blind... but lost!

He who receives the Word of the Kingdom on the good ground is he who hears the word and understands it. These believers bear good fruit in the Kingdom and produce-- some a hundredfold, some sixty, some thirty. They produce the fruit of God's Spirit. As the Scripture reveals, "But the fruit of the Spirit is love, joy, peace, longsuffering, kindness, goodness, faithfulness, gentleness, self-control. Against such there is no law. And those who are Christ's have crucified the flesh with its passions and desires" Galatians 5:22-24 (NKJV). Not only do they bear fruit of the Spirit, but they also minister to those in need. "Dear brothers and sisters, if another believer is overcome by some sin, you who are godly should gently and humbly help that person back onto the right path. And be careful not to fall into the same temptation yourself" Galatians 6:1 (NLT). These Spirit-filled believers hear, see and understand those things which the Spirit is saying to the church. Subsequently, they are able to help others as well as themselves.

JESUS' PARABLES PROPHESIED THE IMMORAL LIFESTYLES OF THE CHURCH!

Many individuals read the Bible, especially Jesus' parables and do not realize that Jesus was simply prophesying the spiritual lives we would live in these last days! The order of Jesus teachings reveals the lifestyles on earth for His followers, the Jewish nation, as well as, those in the body of Christ (the church). Jesus' parables were not only mysteries, but they were secrets kept from the foundation of the world. "All these things Jesus spoke to the multitude in parables; and without a parable He did not speak to them, that it might be fulfilled which was spoken by the prophet, saying: "I will open My mouth in parables; I will utter things kept secret from the foundation of the world" Matthew 13:34-35 (NKJV). His parables were prophecies of the weaknesses and failures of human, sinful flesh. Jesus' prophecies also reveal the manner in which humans would respond to the Gospel and to God's Word. These parables/secrets reveal humankind's physical and spiritual response to the Word of the Kingdom, our strengths and weaknesses, as well as, the manner of our obedience and disobedience. Jesus revealed these things for our benefits so that we would make changes in the spiritual lives and correct those things which offend the Word of God.

During the course of Jesus' ministry, He spoke of the events that were occurring with the Jewish nation and its spiritual leaders. He also prophesied things to come and revealed hidden truths of God's Kingdom on earth. Believers then and now have to be Spirit-filled to unlock the truths of the parables and secrets. Only those individuals who bear God's Spirit are able to obtain the spiritual insight and revelation of His prophesies. Apparently, Jesus wanted those of the Spirit to know not only the escalating levels of false teaching and evil workers that would intrude the church; He also wanted them to know how to enter and/or inherit God's Kingdom. His parables were extremely important to the body of Christ because they revealed the way to God's Kingdom; the criteria to enter and/or inherit the Kingdom; and the immorality that hinders believers from obtaining the Kingdom of God.

In the parable of the wheat and the tares, Jesus spoke of Satan, who came and sowed tares among the wheat and went his way. He said the tares are the sons of the wicked one. As mentioned previously, the tares are Christians who become wicked due to Satan's influence. They serve as pastors, teachers, evangelists, choir members, intercessors, deacons and the like. Jesus reveals their sinful nature and the wicked deeds of these individuals. Just know this is no small thing, but an enormous problem to body of Christ and Christians everywhere! Perhaps I seem to repeat myself many times on various issues, especially the issue of false teachers, etc. I am repetitive with intent, because I want my readers to grasp the important message of this book. Learning theory has proven that a teacher has a better chance of transferring knowledge through repetition. I believe that concept is the reason Jesus taught His message to several disciples who in turn wrote the things He said and did.

Parable of the Mustard Seed!
"And he said whereunto shall we liken the kingdom of God? Or with what com-
parison shall we compare it? It is like a grain of mustard seed, which, when it is
sown in the earth, is less than all the seeds that be in the earth: But when it is sown,
it grows up, and becomes greater than all herbs, and shootout great branches; so
that the fowls of the air may lodge under the shadow of it" Mark 4:30-32 (KJV).

This parable also makes known the significant number of evil workers and
ministers within the body of Christ (the church). Insight to this parable
reveals the grain of a mustard seed grows into an unnaturally large tree.
When the tree grows up and its branches shootout, it harbors the fowl
of the air. The fowl (birds) symbolically represented emissaries of Satan.
"And when he sowed, some seeds fell by the way side, and the fowls came
and devoured them up" Matthew 13:4 (KJV). Metaphorically, the seed
represents the Word of the Kingdom and the fowls are symbolic of false
apostles, false teachers and evil workers that exploit or prey upon others.
They devour God's Word by squandering it, wasting it and teaching fables
instead of the Word of the Kingdom! The growth of the mustard seed
is representative of the kingdom of God (the church). As we know, the
Christian church has expanded all over the world. The Kingdom of God
begins small with the early churches and now has developed into one of the
largest organizations on earth. A large tree harbors many birds. Therefore,
the Kingdom of God (growth of the mustard seed into a large tree) provides
a place, home or habitat for both believers and those who take advantage
of believers. Subsequently, a large conglomerate of false prophets, teachers
and ministers are an intricate part of the church, which is similar to the
multitude of birds lodging in the shadows of a mustard tree. The word
shadow is a metaphor for darkness and the spiritual death of ignorance. It is
the plight of false prophets and teachers as they minister in churches!

Parable of the Leaven!
"Another parable He spoke to them: "The kingdom of heaven is like leaven,
which a woman took and hid in three measures of meal till it was all leav-
ened" Matthew 13:33 (NKJV).

Metaphorically, the word leaven means a chronic display of mental and moral corruption, viewed in its tendency to infect others. In other word, leaven is metaphorically represents the teaching of corrupt doctrine and spiritual errors mixed with truth. This occurs when the pure meat (truth) of the doctrine of Christ has been adulterated with error, resulting in corrupt practice and corrupt doctrine respectively. A little leaven, just like false teaching, corrupts the whole batch or the entire church! Do you not realize that this form of sin is like a little yeast that spreads through the whole batch of dough? Christians should get rid of the *old yeast*.

The Apostle Paul condemns spiritual pride in the church when he condemned a man in a local church who was living in sin with his stepmother. Review the Scriptures below. As Christians, we are warned to take exceptions to these situations. The same applies to church leaders as well!

"I can hardly believe the report about the sexual immorality going on among you—something that even pagans don't do. I am told that a man in your church is living in sin with his stepmother. You are so proud of yourselves, but you should be mourning in sorrow and shame. And you should remove this man from your fellowship.

Even though I am not with you in person, I am with you in the Spirit. And as though I were there, I have already passed judgment on this man in the name of the Lord Jesus. You must call a meeting of the church. I will be present with you in spirit, and so will the power of our Lord Jesus. Then you must throw this man out and hand him over to Satan so that his sinful nature will be destroyed and he himself will be saved on the day the Lord returns.

Your boasting about this is terrible. Don't you realize that this sin is like a little yeast that spreads through the whole batch of dough? Get rid of the old "yeast" by removing this wicked person from among you. Then you will be like a fresh batch of dough made without yeast, which is what you really are. Christ, our Passover Lamb, has been sacrificed for us. So let us celebrate the festival, not with the old bread of wickedness and evil, but with the new bread of sincerity and truth" 1 Corinthians 5:1-8 (NLT).

Similar to the parable of the mustard seed, a mustard seed grows into a great tree which harbors a lot of birds. The Body of Christ (the universal church) is equally a sanctuary for a conglomerate of false prophets and teachers. As you might imagine, many believers are deceived and lost because of their false doctrine and distorted ways!

Parable of the Pearl of Great Price!
"Again, the kingdom of heaven is like a merchant seeking beautiful pearls, who, when he had found one pearl of great price, went and sold all that he had and bought it" Matthew 13:45-46 (NKJV).

In this parable, a merchant is considered a person on a journey who is seeking beautiful pearls. Seeking is craving or demanding something from someone. Seeking is to *seek or strive after, to endeavor and desire.* Now the King James states the merchant is seeking goodly pearls instead of beautiful pearls. Goodly means beautiful by reason of purity of heart and life, and hence praiseworthy. It is morally good, noble, honorable and conferring honor. God is essentially, absolutely and consummately _good_. To seek God and our Lord Jesus Christ is the greatest venture to endeavor!

Notice that the merchant stopped seeking the goodly pearls once he found the pearl of great price. In the natural, the pearl of great price is something of great value that can be bought and sold for a great sum of money. Unfortunately, too many in the body of Christ are seeking items of great monetary value to obtain wealth and to appear important in the world's eyes. Spiritually speaking, the pearl of great price is our Lord Jesus Christ who is the source for obtaining eternal life and the promised inheritance of our Father. The great price is that which was paid by Jesus for our redemption. He emptied Himself of His glory; came to the earth in the form of a lowly servant; and shed His precious blood on the cross for the sins of the world. A great price is also found in the tribulations and sufferings we must endure to enter the Kingdom of God.

In these this parable, the pearl is not easily obtained which indicates that spiritual truth and insight are required by Christians to enter God's Kingdom. This truth is not found in our intelligence, physical power or worldly wisdom. The mysteries of the Kingdom of heaven are hidden from those who are unable to hear, see and comprehend within their hearts. It is because disobediences, the natural consequences of their unbelief, produce spiritual blindness. Furthermore, the natural person cannot understand the things of the Spirit for they are foolish to him or her.

> *"However, we speak wisdom among those who are mature, yet not the wisdom of this age, nor of the rulers of this age, who are coming to nothing. But we speak the wisdom of God in a mystery, the hidden wisdom which God ordained before the ages for our glory, which none of the rulers of this age knew; for had they known, they would not have crucified the Lord of glory.*
>
> *But as it is written: "Eye has not seen, nor ear heard, nor have entered into the heart of man the things which God has prepared for those who love Him." But God has revealed them to us through His Spirit. For the Spirit searches all things, yes, the deep things of God. For what man knows the things of a man except the spirit of the man which is in him? Even so no one knows the things of God except the Spirit of God. Now we have received, not the spirit of the world, but the Spirit who is from God, that we might know the things that have been freely given to us by God.*
>
> *These things we also speak, not in words which man's wisdom teaches but which the Holy Spirit teaches, comparing spiritual things with spiritual. But the natural man does not receive the things of the Spirit of God, for they are foolishness to him; nor can he know them, because they are <u>spiritually discerned</u>"* 1 Corinthians 2:6-14 (NKJV).

God has freely given faithful and obedient believers the power to endure and to overcome all the circumstances of life and of the enemy. However, the wisdom and knowledge to partake of these gifts, talents, abilities and spiritual understanding only comes to humans by the Holy Spirit. For the Spirit not only comforts, but it endows believers with the spiritual wisdom from God. The door to the Holy Spirit is through Jesus Christ whom we believe in. The door to Jesus is acquired through loving and trusting Jesus, as well as, faith and obedience to Him. *It comes no other way!* Many have forgotten the things human flesh must do to receive the promised blessing of God. In no way can believers continue to allow the lust and desires of their flesh to dominate them!

Parable of the Dragnet!
"Again, the kingdom of heaven is like a dragnet that was cast into the sea and gathered some of every kind, which, when it was full, they drew to shore; and they sat down and gathered the good into vessels, but threw the bad away. So it will be at the end of the age. The angels will come forth, separate the wicked from among the just, and cast them into the furnace of fire. There will be wailing and gnashing of teeth."

Jesus said to them, "Have you understood all these things?" They said to Him, "Yes, Lord. Then He said to them, "Therefore every scribe instructed concerning the kingdom of heaven is like a householder who brings out of his treasure things new and old" Matthew 13:47-52 (NKJV).

This parable is similar to the parable of the wheat and the tares. It is because both parables reveal the method in which the Kingdom of God speaks of those who have given their lives to the cause of God. One parable symbolically presents God's people as wheat and tares. The other parable presents God's people as some of every kind. Presumably a fish of every kind! In this parable, the fish of every kind (God's people) are gathered together or allowed to live together until separation time. Separation time is at the end of the age when the angels will come forth, separate the wicked from among the just, and cast them into the furnace of fire. There will be wailing and gnashing of teeth. The important thing to understand and embrace is that Jesus' angels will gather out of His kingdom all things that *offend* and *those who practice lawlessness* and will cast them into the furnace of fire. A person's evil deeds can be lived out without any exposure or vindication until the Day of Judgment, because God allows the good and the bad to live together until separation time. But trust the Word; it reveals that He *will not* allow those who offend and practice lawlessness to inherit God's Kingdom.

"Do you not know that the unrighteous will not inherit the kingdom of God? Do not be deceived. Neither fornicators, nor idolaters, nor adulterers, nor

homosexuals, nor sodomites, nor thieves, nor covetous, nor drunkards, nor revilers, nor extortionists will inherit the kingdom of God" 1 *Corinthians 6:9-10 (NKJV).*

It is important to note that the parable describes the people and events that occur in the Kingdom of heaven and the results of people's actions and lifestyles. The parable refers to the Kingdom of God and *not the evilness in the world* because the world already has its reward. The revelation of all parables refers to Christians whom the royal power and dignity has been conferred upon in the Messiah's kingdom. Jesus wants His people to understand the iniquities that occur with God's elect and how they must compel their own hearts to seek after truth, love, faith and obedience in order to inherit the Kingdom. Judgment comes to those *who offend* and to those *who practice lawlessness.* An offense is any impediment placed in the way and causing one to stumble or fall, (a stumbling block) i.e. a rock which is a cause of stumbling. A stumbling block is the spiritual hindrance to another by a selfish use of liberty. Metaphorically, it is doing anything to lead astray Jews, Greeks or Christians in a way that is arousing prejudice or becoming a hindrance to others or causing them to fall by the wayside.

There are many in God's Kingdom that offend and cause others to stumble and to fall away. I am not saying their deception is deliberate, but it occurs nevertheless. Individuals who lead people astray today are like the scribes and Pharisees of Jesus' day. Their hearts are fixed on traditions and lusts that cause them to be dishonest and blind. Scribes, through their traditions, instead of being moral and spiritual help, became an instrument for *preventing* true access to God. Jesus told the scribes and Pharisees that they shut-up God's Kingdom by not excepting Him or the message of the Kingdom. "But woe to you, scribes and Pharisees, hypocrites! For you shut up the kingdom of heaven against men; for you neither go in yourselves, nor do you allow those who are entering to go in" Matthew 23:13 (NKJV).

The apostle Peter said, "But there were also false prophets among the people, even as there will be false teachers among you, who will secretly bring in destructive heresies, even denying the Lord who bought them, and bring on themselves swift destruction" 2 Peter 2:1 (NKJV). Today's ministers of false origin do not deny Jesus and His Kingdom with their words, but they fail to obey His assignment to preach the Kingdom message and to reveal its mysteries and secrets. These individuals prefer to preach and teach the life of Christ over and over again and Old Testament fables and blessings that can come to Christians. Much of their ministry reveals truth from the Bible, but it's now time to move on from these perils and progress forward.

> *"So let us stop going over the basic teachings about Christ again and again. Let us go on instead and become mature in our understanding. Surely we don't need to start again with the fundamental importance of repenting from evil deeds and placing our faith in God. You don't need further instruction about baptisms, the laying on of hands, and the resurrection of the dead and eternal judgment. And so, God willing, we will move forward to further understanding" Hebrews 6:1-3 (NLT)*

Now is the time to reveal the mysteries of the Kingdom and tell it like it is! Those who practice lawlessness and/or iniquity will also be casted into the furnace of fire at separation time. Those who do iniquity is everyone that *practices* sin (not just the committal of an act) because sin is lawlessness. It is the contempt and violation of law, iniquity, wickedness which denotes unrighteousness. It is a condition of not being right, whether with God, according to the standard of His holiness and righteousness, or with man, according to the standard of what man knows to be right by his conscience and the law of the land. Lawlessness, on the other hand is where the thought is not simply that of doing what is unlawful, but of flagrant defiance of the known will of God. This definition of sin sets forth its essential character as the rejection of the law, or will, of God and the substitution of the will of self.

This parable speaks to the separation of the wicked from among the just and how the wicked will be cast into the furnace of fire. More importantly, it speaks to those who offend and cause others to stumble! Jesus said, "Therefore every scribe *instructed* concerning the kingdom of heaven is like a householder who brings out of his treasure of things new and old" Matthew 13:52 (NKJV). Every teacher of religious law who becomes a disciple, teacher or minister in the Kingdom of Heaven is like a home-owner who brings from his storeroom new gems of truth as well as old. A homeowner is the one in charge and responsible for all that goes on in the house. Therefore, those who are taught in the mysteries of the Gospel and have to teach others, is like a homeowner who brings forth or gives out of his/her treasure God's divine truth.

They are responsible to teach those things they hear from God's Spirit, which is relevant for today! However, many are given to shape their messages to the paradigm of their ministry. In other words, many research the Scriptures to teach about wealth and prosperity rather than teach the full council of God. These individuals are those who offend the house of God and cause many to stumble. The Lord still speaks to humans through the Holy Spirit and it is imperative to hear those things which are relevant instead of the things which please the lust of the flesh. Many teachers are stuck on traditional messages or messages of the flesh rather than those things God's Spirit is saying to the church. They should be like the house-holder who brings out of his treasure of knowledge Divine words from the Lord which is both old and new!

Jesus Reveals the Wickedness and Spiritual Blindness Within The Body of Christ (The Church)!

As Jesus spoke parables to His followers, the multitude, He also proph-esied these mysteries to all future generations. Jesus' parables are of extreme importance because they are the mysteries of the Kingdom of Heaven which are only given to those who see, hear and understand by God's Spirit! In other words, only those who are Spirit-filled are given to know the mysteries of God just like Jesus disciples. These myster-ies are the secret counsels which are governed by God in dealing with the righteous; they are revealed only to the godly and hidden from the ungodly.

"All these things Jesus spoke to the multitude in parables; and without a parable He did not speak to them, that it might be fulfilled which was spoken by the prophet, saying: "I will open My mouth in parables; I will utter things kept secret from the foundation of the world" Matthew 13:34-35 (NKJV). All of Jesus' parables were prophetic utterances spoken by Him to those who are seeking and pressing through to life in God's Kingdom, willing to endure the hardships and afflictions of this world.

These parables reveal the wickedness of humans, the cause of human wickedness and the spiritual blindness that so many of His followers experience. The order in which Jesus taught the parables represented the way of life God's people would live on the earth. The parable chronicled their lives, their beliefs, and deceptions, lack of understanding, hardness of their hearts, spiritual blindness and more! They also revealed the methods in which humans could be delivered from the bondage of corruption and how they could become Spirited-filled and obedience believers. Jesus prophesied all the events that would occur in the life of humans on the earth, both good and bad! Jesus prophesied His rejection and the rejection of God's Kingdom. He also prophesied the multitude of false prophets and teachers that would emerge and the spiritual blindness of God's people. It is for these reasons that many offend and practice lawlessness. Therefore, only a few will *find life* in The Kingdom of God.

As mentioned earlier, Jesus parables prophesied the spiritual blindness and satanic mixture in the body of Christ (the church)! Being aware of what Jesus said and in the order He said it gives you tremendous insight as to how the body of Christ lives on this earth. It is not a pretty picture because so many Christians live below the standards God's predestination established for them. These mysteries (parables) *do reveal* to Spirit-filled believers a clear message of what they must do to be saved. Let us review once more the essence of the parables Jesus gave.

- **The Parable of the sower** – Jesus' parable validates the prophecy of Isaiah which established that Jesus' followers, both during His ministry on earth and in future generations, would become spiritually blind! Jesus recounted the prophecy and said, "Hearing you will hear and shall not understand, and seeing you will see and not perceive; for the hearts of this people have grown dull" Matthew 13:15 (NKJV). Only those who live according to God's Spirit have the spiritual prowess to hear and know what the Spirit is saying to the church. Therefore, a multitude of Jews and Christians are spiritually blind and need to surrender *the will of their soul* to the power of God's Spirit in order to be saved!

- **The Parable of the Wheat and the Tares** – Jesus revealed the spiritual mixture that would occur in His body, the body of Christ (the church). He made known the tremendous proliferation of false apostles and deceitful workers that would plague the church of God by transforming themselves into apostles of righteousness. Even Satan would transform himself into an angel of light. This occurs in the church while God's people *sleep*. To sleep is to yield to sloth and sin and to be indifferent to one's salvation. Jesus stated to let them live together until the end of the age when God's angels will separate those who offend and practice lawlessness from those who were obedient, faithful and lived according to God's Spirit.

- **The Parable of the Mustard Seed** – This parable is a metaphor of how a small mustard seed grows into a large tree that supports a multitude of birds in comparison to the growth of universal church that is overwhelmed with false apostles, false doctrines and deceitful workers. Jesus gives us a visual image of the level of false prophets and /or teachers by describing a tree full of birds who are the adversaries of the cross. The level or amount of your adversaries is many. "Be sober, be vigilant; because your adversary the devil walks about like a roaring lion, seeking whom he may devour" 1 Peter 5:8 (NKJV). The amount of false prophets and ministers is the reason so many apostles like Matthew, Mark, Luke, Paul, Titus, Peter and Jude warned us against false teachings in the last days.

- **The Parable of the Leaven** – One may ask of himself/herself how the church of God could be beset with so many false ministers and teachers of God's Word who are teaching false doctrine and/or fables. Jesus gives the parable of the leaven to show that it only takes a little leaven to leaven an entire batch of meal. Subsequently, it only took a few false prophets to defile the entire body of Christ (the church). This caused a proliferation of evil workers to occur!

- **The Parables of the Hidden Treasure and Pearl of Great Price** – As we have seen, Jesus' parables reveal the effects of God's curse on humans. Because God's creation was disobedient in the garden, God subjected His creation to vanity and futility, not willingly, but in hopes that humans would become obedient. Through suffering, they would come to know, love and believe in Jesus and allow the power of God's Spirit to deliver them from the bondage of corruption that produced their sinful nature (sinful flesh). Jesus made known the essence of the corruption in humans, the deception of Satan and his demons, and the lust of human flesh in many of His parables. However, only Spirit-filled believers would be given to know the revelation and spiritual insight of the parables. Therefore, only Spirit-filled individuals would know to seek God's Kingdom and the way of the cross. _The way of the cross_ is the suffering humans take on as members of Christ's body. Know this, the parables did not only describe the wickedness, perversion and iniquity of humans, but they also revealed the character and purpose of those who receive Jesus in their heart and make Him preeminent in their lives!

Such is the case with the two parables, the Hidden Treasure and Pearl of Great Price. Both parables involve a man who sold all he had to possess the kingdom. The treasure and the pearl represent Jesus Christ and the salvation He offers. In both parables, the treasures are hidden; spiritual truth will be missed by many and cannot be found by intelligence or power or worldly wisdom, but only by spiritual knowledge! Believe me, there are individuals in this world who have become partakers of the Holy Spirit, have tasted the good Word of God and of the powers of the age to come, and have surrendered all to Jesus and have made Him their pearl of great joy! I know because I am one of those believers. It is almost impossible to describe the joy and peace one gets when Jesus is not only your Lord and Savior, but He is your *all in all!* Nothing else comes before Him in your life! Not your wife, your family, friends, occupation, home, cars, entertainment--*nothing!* There is pure joy and peace in individuals that surrender to Jesus and to the power of His might in spite of the perversion in this world and its tribulation! *Nothing else in this world compares to Him!*

CHAPTER 4

Embrace the Weapons God gives to Faitheful Believes!

TAKE THE KINGDOM OF GOD BY FORCE!

THE APOSTLE PAUL ADVISED TIMOTHY in 2 Timothy 3:12 (NKJV) - "Yes, and all who *desire* to live godly in Christ Jesus will suffer persecution." Subsequently, those who seek God's Kingdom will suffer many hardships, anguish, burdens, distress, persecution, tribulation, troubles, afflictions, trials, tests, sorrows and sufferings as record in Acts. "After preaching the Good News in Derbe and making many disciples, Paul and Barnabas returned to Lustra, Iconium, and Antioch of Pisidia, where they strengthened the believers. They encouraged them to continue in the faith, reminding them that we must *suffer many hardships* to enter the Kingdom of God" Acts 14:21-22 (NLT). I realize this may be different from the messages you have heard, that God's people must suffer tribulations, but it is the true Word of God!

God set forth His will on earth to obtain children. Those who become His children must be worthy citizens of His Kingdom. Because the beginning of human life on the earth started with disobedience; He established a form of living that would bring God's elect into obedience. That form of living was the curse! The earth was cursed to produce hardships, tribulations, afflictions, trials, tests, sorrows and sufferings in the lives of God's people. This suffering would accomplish two things. First, it would test the faith of those who professed Him as their Lord and Savior and who would love and obey Him. Secondly, suffering on the earth would bring about obedience. Yes, we learn obedience by the things we suffer just like Jesus did while He was on earth in the flesh. "Though He was a Son, yet He learned obedience by the things which He suffered" Hebrews 5:8 (NKJV). Jesus did not learn obedience as the Savior of this world as a Spirit being because He delighted in constant obedience to the Father's will. He learned obedience as a *flesh being.* This meant that true believers learn obedience by pressing through the trials and burdens of this earth to become worthy children of God. Remember God's Words in the Garden of Eden, "Cursed is the ground for your sake; in toil you shall eat of it all the days of your life. Both thorns and thistles it shall bring forth for you, and you shall eat the herb of the field" Genesis 3:17-18 (NKJV).

The reason this insight may seem strange to you is because you are, perhaps, seeing and hearing it for the first time. As I have said so many times before, many of today's church leaders minister to the *flesh* of converts by preaching the planting of a seed (money) to reap a harvest. They also constantly focus on God's blessings and when the believer can reap them. This style ministry *stimulates the desires* of human flesh which diametrically opposes living before the Lord as a living sacrifice, holy and acceptable to Him. "I beseech you therefore, brethren, by the mercies of God, that you present your bodies a living sacrifice, holy, acceptable to God, which is your reasonable service. And do not be conformed to this world, but be transformed by the renewing of your mind, that you may prove what is that good and acceptable and perfect will of God" Romans 12:1-2 (NKJV). Yes, the Lord blesses our lives with things of this world such as wealth, spiritual gifts, worldly talents and more. However, these blessings coincide with the advancement of His Kingdom, and He expects the believer to bear good fruit with the blessings he/she receives.

Regrettably, the sinful nature of human flesh oftentimes *desires and lusts* for the things of this world and the deceitfulness of its riches. Jesus said, "Now he who received seed among the thorns is he who hears the word, and the cares of this world and the deceitfulness of riches choke the word, and he becomes unfruitful" Matthew 13:22 (NKJV). This is the reason there is a constant battle between human flesh and God's Spirit for the control of our souls. "For the flesh lusts against the Spirit, and the Spirit against the flesh; and these are contrary to one another, so that you do not do the things that you wish" Galatians 5:17 (NKJV). Prosperity preaching causes the human flesh to seek after wealth, abundance, afflu-ence, success; control, overabundance and unsatisfied wants! The sinful nature of our flesh is the overriding problem of God's people on earth. It has prevented many people from being obedient to God's Word.

"Those who are dominated by the sinful nature think about sinful things, but those who are controlled by the Holy Spirit think about things that please the Spirit. So letting your sinful nature control your mind leads to death. But letting the Spirit control your mind leads to life and peace. For the sinful nature is always hostile to God. It never did obey God's laws, and it never will. That's why those who are still under the control of their sinful nature can never please God" Romans 8:5-8 (NLT). Teaching a gospel that stimulates the flesh *to want* more and more instead of seeking God's Kingdom and it sacrifices, simply opposes the Word of the Kingdom. Those who seek God's Kingdom realize that they must take on the sufferings of Christ and press forward into God's Kingdom through hardships, sorrows and sufferings, to live according to God's will.

Jesus said, "And from the days of John the Baptist until now the kingdom of heaven suffers violence, and the violent take it by force" Matthew 11:12 (NKJV). It means, from the day Jesus taught the Word of the Kingdom until now many have been *pressing to enter it.* Taking the Kingdom by force is when you press forward with all your heart to enter the Kingdom with the help of the Holy Spirit. This chapter defines the *violence* believers must embrace, what it means to *take it by force* and by whose power the individual *takes* the Kingdom of God.

God's Kingdom is where faithful believers find *life* on earth and/or inherit *eternal life* hereafter. However, that *life* comes with a *price.* Jesus said, "Therefore do not worry, saying, 'What shall we eat?' or 'What shall we drink?' or 'What shall we wear?' For after all these things the Gentiles seek. For your heavenly Father knows that you need all these things. But seek first the kingdom of God and His righteousness, and all these things shall be added to you. Therefore do not worry about tomorrow, for tomorrow will worry about its own things. Sufficient for the day is its own trouble" Matthew 6:31-34 (NKJV). God's righteousness is the state of a believer who is as he ought to be, righteous--the condition acceptable to

God. It is those who seek the doctrine concerning the way in which man may attain a state approved of God. It is the integrity, virtue, purity of life, rightness, correctness of thinking feeling, and acting. Having its own trouble denotes the evil that causes labor, pain, sorrow or malignant evil. Hence, today's trouble is enough for today.

THE KINGDOM IS TAKEN FORCEFULLY BY THOSE WHO HUNGER AND THIRST FOR GOD'S RIGHTEOUSNESS!

It seems strange to say that the kingdom of heaven suffers violence and the violent take it by force until one understands the complete revelation of what this means. In other words, "The law and the prophets were until John. Since that time the kingdom of God has been preached, and everyone is pressing into it" Luke 16:16 (NKJV). Pressing into the Kingdom are those who are possessed of eagerness and zeal. Instead of yielding to the opposition of religious foes, such as the scribes, Pharisees and false ministers of today, true believers ae pressing their way into the kingdom and possessing it. Today, Christians must take God's Kingdom by forcing themselves past the _perils_ of false teaching to obtain the truth of God's Word and enduring many tribulations. They must be like John the Baptist when he pressed passed the objections of the scribes and Pharisees to teach and baptize those who followed him.

The Kingdom of God has many adversaries that oppose the spiritual advancement of God's chosen people (Jews and Christians). As we know, many of these adversaries are used by God to bless, develop and mature His children, through sufferings! Such was the case with Joseph and his brothers.

> *"When Joseph's brothers saw that their father was dead, they said, "Perhaps Joseph will hate us, and may actually repay us for all the evil which we did to him." So they sent messengers to Joseph, saying, "Before your father died he commanded, saying, 'thus you shall say to Joseph: "I beg you, please forgive the trespass of your brothers and their sin; for they did evil to you."' Now, please, forgive the trespass of the servants of the God of your father." And Joseph wept when they spoke to him.*

Then his brothers also went and fell down before his face, and they said, "Behold, we are your servants." Joseph said to them, "Do not be afraid, for am I in the place of God? But as for you, you meant evil against me; but God meant it for good, in order to bring it about as it is this day, to save many people alive. Now therefore, do not be afraid; I will provide for you and your little ones. And he comforted them and spoke kindly to them" Genesis 50:15-21 (NKJV).

Satan is one who comes to kill, steal and destroy! "Then Jesus said to them again, "Most assuredly, I say to you, I am the door of the sheep. All who ever came before Me are thieves and robbers, but the sheep did not hear them. I am the door. If anyone enters by Me, he will be saved, and will go in and out and find pasture. The thief does not come except to steal, and to kill, and to destroy. I have come that they may have life and that they may have it more abundantly" John 10:7-10 (NKJV). As believers, we must press through, overcome and endure to the end. Jesus said in Matthew 24:13 (NKJV) – "But he who endures to the end shall be saved." For the purpose of identifying why it is necessary to *take the Kingdom by force* and press into it, the following situations reveal the many adversaries and/or hindrances that attempt to prevent the cause of God on earth and the establishment of His Kingdom.

FALSE PROPHETS AND RELIGIOUS LEADERS SHUT-UP THE WAY TO GOD'S KINGDOM!

As mentioned earlier in the book, the scribes and the Pharisees were the false teachers of Jesus' day. These leaders and the false prophets and teachers of today are the same! They shut-up the way to God's Kingdom. Jesus said, "But woe to you, scribes and Pharisees, hypocrites! For you shut up the kingdom of heaven against men; for you neither go in yourselves, nor do you allow those who are entering to go in" Matthew 23:13 (NKJV). They are like unthinking animals, creatures of instinct, born to be caught and destroyed. They scoff at things they do not understand and teach things that tinkle the ears of parishioners for high financial rewards! Their destruction is their reward for the harm they do. They love to indulge in evil pleasures and they delight in deception. They commit adultery with both their eyes and with their bodies. Jesus said, "Hypocrites! Well did Isaiah prophesy about you, saying: 'These people draw near to Me with their mouth, and honor Me with their lips, but their heart is far from Me. And in vain they worship Me, teaching as doctrines *the commandments of men*" Matthew 15:7-9 (NKJV).

FAITHFUL BELIEVERS PRESS FORWARD TO THE KINGDOM OF GOD!

Salvation does not come without obligations, strife and suffering! This is why one must *press* into God's Kingdom by enduring and overcoming the challenges of life. God gave us His Spirit to comfort us through these trials. Paul advised those in Philippi that, "Not that I have already attained, or am already perfected; but I press on, that I may lay hold of that for which Christ Jesus has also laid hold of me. Brethren, I do not count myself to have apprehended; but one thing I do, forgetting those things which are behind and reaching forward to those things which are ahead, I press toward the goal for the prize of the upward call of God in Christ Jesus. Therefore let us, as many as are mature, have this mind; and if in anything you think otherwise, God will reveal even this to you. Nevertheless, to the degree that we have already attained, let us walk by the same rule, let us be of the same mind" Philippians 3:12-16 (NKJV).

There are many obstacles believers must engage to enter God's Kingdom. Some of these obstacles represent God's will in the believer's life while others do not! Obstacles, such as tribulations, afflictions, deception and the Lord's chastisements may hinder and/or cause difficulty in the believer's life, but those who endure will be saved. For the obstacles themselves can yield a peaceable fruit of righteousness to those who are being *trained* by them. Please do not forget, one must go through many tribulations to enter the kingdom of God. Paul said, "Strengthening the souls of the disciples, exhorting them to continue in the faith, and saying, "We must through many tribulations enter the kingdom of God" Acts 14:22 (NKJV). These tribulations represent the difficulties in life that Christians face. The New Living Translations records the word *hardship* instead of the word *tribulation*; however, they both mean the same.

Metaphorically, the tribulations recorded in Acts are the oppressions, afflictions, trials, distresses and other difficult situations God's people experience. Believers everywhere must experience these afflictions as part of God's Divine will for His people! "So be truly glad. There is wonderful joy ahead, even though you must endure many trials for a little while. These trials will show that your faith is genuine. It is being tested as fire tests and purifies gold—though your faith is far more precious than mere gold. So when your faith remains strong through many trials, it will bring you much praise and glory and honor on the day when Jesus Christ is revealed to the whole world. You love him even though you have never seen him. Though you do not see him now, you trust him; and you rejoice with a glorious, inexpressible joy. The reward for trusting him will be the salvation of your souls" 1 Peter 1:6-9 (NLT). Always remember, God's people learn *obedience* by the things we suffer! The Holy Spirit gives the saints of God the ability to endure suffering and overcome the tribulations of this world!

Another major obstacle in the life of Christians is the wiles of Satan. The wiles of Satan are stratagems or tricks intended to deceive or ensnare believers. They are performed in a disarming or seductive manner using a craft, a device or a procedure to deceive and/or trick humans. Please know that God's people were called to endure and overcome the tribulations and tragedies of this world. Many Christians believe we have the authority and the ability to rebuke, blind and defeat Satan. However, Satan was given the authority to disrupt the life of humans as in the case with Job. Faithful believers have the *ability and power*, through the Holy Spirit, to *resist the devil* and see him go away! "Therefore submit to God. Resist the devil and he will flee from you" James 4:7 (NKJV). There is a plethora of other weapons God gives us to successfully endure and overcome various forces and situations in our spiritual lives. They are available, but few Christians actually use them to the extent and *measure* that is available.

Embrace the Weapons God's Gives His People!

Because of man's disobedience in the Garden of Eden, humans became sinful flesh endowed with weaknesses. Therefore, humans became prey to the onslaught of Satan and his angels. God saw the weakness of human flesh; everything they thought or imagined was consistently and totally *evil*. "Then the LORD saw that the wickedness of man was great in the earth, and that every intent of the thoughts of his heart was only evil continually" Genesis 6:5 (NKJV). As humans lived under the law, the thoughts and imaginations of their hearts was continually evil.

However, God sent His Son, Jesus Christ to deliver us from this bondage of corruption which led to human death. Through Jesus, we can now be renewed in the spirit of our mind and become the *individuals* who were created according to the will of God, in true righteousness and holiness. "But you have not so learned Christ, if indeed you have heard Him and have been taught by Him, as the truth is in Jesus: that you put off, concerning your former conduct, the old man which grows corrupt according to the deceitful lusts, and be renewed in the spirit of your mind, and that you put on the new man which was created according to God, in *true righteousness and holiness*" Ephesians 4:20-24 (NKJV). *Do you understand what this Scripture means?* Through Jesus Christ and the power of God's Spirit, humankind can return to the way God created us, which is in true righteousness and holiness. Of course, it can only be done by and through the power of Jesus Christ and God's Spirit. Human flesh, separated from God's power cannot accomplish righteousness or holiness. It is because flesh itself cannot please God. "So then, those who are in the flesh cannot please God" Romans 8:8 (NKJV). For in the flesh, nothing good dwells! "For I know that in me (that is, in my flesh) nothing good dwells; for to will is present with me, but how to perform what is good I do not find" Romans 7:18 (NKJV).

Even though human flesh will encounter tribulations and sufferings due to the curse, we do not *have to war* according to the flesh! God called us to present our bodies a living sacrifice, holy, acceptable to God. Living sacrificially, God's people are victims of the cross like Jesus Christ. Humans become victims because we learn obedience through the things we suffer just like Jesus did while in the flesh. "Though He was a Son, yet He learned obedience by the things which He suffered" Hebrews 5:8 (NKJV). As we suffer, our consolation abounds through Christ. "For as the sufferings of Christ abound in us, so our consolation also abounds through Christ" Corinthians 1:5 (NKJV). We may encounter suffering, but God will not allow us to be tempted more than we can bear. "No temptation has overtaken you except such as is common to man; but God is faithful, who will not allow you to be *tempted* beyond what you are able, but with the temptation will also make the way of escape, that you may be able to bear it" 1 Corinthians 10:13 (NKJV). Being tempted is of God, and it means to inflict evils upon someone in order to prove character and steadfastness of faith.

We may have to endure and overcome many adversities and sufferings in our lives, but we still do not have to live as perverted and ungodly individuals in this world. We humans have the power through God's Spirit to rise above ungodly sins by the renewing of our minds. "And do not be conformed to this world, but be transformed by the renewing of your mind, that you may prove what is that good and acceptable and perfect will of God" Romans 12:2 (NKJV). Faithful believers have the ability and power, through the Holy Spirit, to pull down strongholds, cast down arguments and every high thing that exalts itself against the knowledge of God. "For though we walk in the flesh, we do not war according to the flesh. For the weapons of our warfare are not carnal but mighty in God for pulling down strongholds, casting down arguments and every high thing that exalts itself against the knowledge of God, bringing every thought into captivity to the obedience of Christ, and being ready to punish all disobedience when your obedience is fulfilled" 2 Corinthians 10:3-6 (NKJV).

The Apostle Paul said, "But there is another power [law] within me that is at war with my mind. This power makes me a slave to the sin that is still within me" Romans 7:23 (NLT). The law of my mind is that principle which governs the new nature of believers in virtue (morally good behavior or character) of their new birth. The law of sin is the principle by which sin exerts its influence and power despite the desire to do what is right. In other words, even though believers are born-again, there is a principle (a basic belief, theory, or rule that has a major influence on the way in which something is done or the way someone lives) that wars *with* the mind which can keep God's people in slavery to sin. It is a spiritual conflict which only the Holy Spirit can give us power over! However, a believer must crave, desire, and press their heart for a change as they seek God's kingdom and His righteousness. Seeking God's Kingdom is asking for citizenship with all your heart, soul and mind!

The reason many have not asked is because they do not sincerely desire nor hunger to change! Many Christians are comfortable with the sin in their lives and have no desire to change. Whenever they do ask the Lord for something, many ask for the things that pleasure them such as entertainment, larger homes, new automobiles, a non-believing soul mate and much more! The writer of James gave insight to this matter.

"Where do wars and fights come from among you? Do they not come from your desires for pleasure that war in your members? You lust and do not have. You murder and covet and cannot obtain. You fight and war. Yet you do not have because you do not ask. You ask and do not receive, because you ask amiss, that you may spend it on your pleasures. Adulterers and adulteresses! Do you not know that friendship with the world is enmity with God? Whoever therefore wants to be a friend of the world makes himself an enemy of God. Or do you think that the Scripture says in vain, "The Spirit who dwells in us yearns jealously" James 4:1-5 (NKJV)?

The following definitions will assist you in understanding the Scriptures above. The word *amiss* means *out of proper order.* There are Christians who passively attend church and passively become involved in the things of God. The word passively means not being active or not participating perceptibly. Some Christians are asking "out of order" because their hearts are not actively participating in promoting God's Kingdom. These individuals pray and ask for things that benefit their own selfish desires.

Definition of *God's weapon* – As mentioned in the Scripture, "For the weapons of our warfare are not carnal but mighty in God for pulling down strongholds, casting down arguments and every high thing that exalts itself against the knowledge of God bringing every thought into captivity to the obedience of Christ, and being ready to punish all disobedience when your obedience is fulfilled" 2 Corinthians 10:3-6 (NKJV). God's weapons are our *spiritual* helps for overcoming the temptations of the devil.

- **Armor of light** – Metaphorically, this phrase means spiritual enlightenment produced by the Holy Spirit.
- **Armor of righteousness** – "We prove ourselves by our purity, our understanding, our patience, our kindness, by the Holy Spirit within us, and by our sincere love. We faithfully preach the truth. God's power is working in us. We use the weapons of righteousness in the right hand for attack and the left hand for defense" Corinthians 6:6-7 (NLT).
- **Weapons of Christian warfare** – The weapons of our warfare are not carnal like having the nature of flesh, i.e. under the control of the animal appetites. But they are powerful and able to work, to carry spiritual things into effect. "Now may the God of hope fill you with all joy and peace in believing, that you may abound in hope by the power of the Holy Spirit" Romans 15:13 (NKJV). The Holy Spirit gives power to the believer to pull down strongholds in our lives that are dominated by evil powers and principalities. He gives power to cast down arguments which is are angry disagreements; and imagination is the faculty of thinking, knowing and understanding. Subsequently, the believer is then able to cast down every thought (a purpose, device of the mind) and every high thing that exalts itself against the knowledge of God. Pulling down strongholds metaphorically denotes a stronghold or fortress of those things in which mere human confidence is imposed (to establish as something to be obeyed or complied with).

Believers do not have to remain in bondage to the thoughts of their heart because the power of the Holy Spirit can deliver them from these thoughts. However, one must seek God's Kingdom; submit to the control of God's Spirit and cherish the power from on high! That power is committed to those who have become believers, are empowered by the Spirit of God, are indwelt by Him, and will exercise the Spirit's power for God's glory. Believers should bring every thought (The faculty of thinking or reasoning) into captivity (subjugating every thought) to the obedience of Christ. Be ready to punish all disobedience (refusal or failure to obey) when your obedience is fulfilled. *The Holy Spirit gives God's saints the ability* to use many weapons of warfare to pull down strongholds, cast down arguments and every high thing that exalts itself against the knowledge of God. Remember, God saw that the greatest weakness of humans was in everything they thought or imagined, and it was consistently and totally *evil*. Now we have no obligation to do what our sinful nature urges us to do. "The righteous requirement of the law can be fulfilled in us who do not walk according to the flesh but according to the Spirit" Romans 8:4 (NKJV). Subsequently, by God's Spirit, we are free from indwelling sin! "There is therefore now no condemnation to those who are in Christ Jesus, who do not walk according to the flesh, but according to the Spirit" Romans 8:1 (NKJV). Christians who live according to God's Spirit are not condemned whenever they commit an occasional sin.

THE WHOLE ARMOR OF GOD!

As Christians, we know that Satan comes to kill, to steal and to destroy the lives of God's people. We also know that Satan is an evil spirit as the god of this world that uses deception to *confuse* and *influence* God's people to lust after the things of this world instead of seeking God as a living sacrifice. However, to those who love the Lord and are called according to His purposes, God has given them armor to endure and overcome the wiles of Satan. God's people *must use* this armor in order to reject the devil and make him flee from them. Hence, believers must do more than just know about the armor and talk about the armor; they also must use *the component parts* of the armor for the armor to be effective! God's armor is shown below. Therefore, put on the whole armor, not just part of the armor of God, in order to become faithful and worthy Christians.

"Finally, my brethren, be strong in the Lord and in the power of His might. Put on the whole armor of God that you may be able to stand against the wiles of the devil. For we do not wrestle against flesh and blood, but against principalities, against powers, against the rulers of the darkness of this age, against spiritual hosts of wickedness in the heavenly places. Therefore take up the whole armor of God that you may be able to withstand in the evil day, and having done all, to stand.

Stand therefore, having girded your waist with truth, having put on the breastplate of righteousness, and having shod your feet with the preparation of the gospel of peace; above all, taking the shield of faith with which you will be able to quench all the fiery darts of the wicked one. And take the helmet of salvation, and the sword of the Spirit, which is the word of God; praying always with all prayer and supplication in the Spirit, being watchful to this end with all perseverance and supplication for all the saints" Ephesians 6:10-18 (NKJV).

Many Christians are willing to pray and to be watchful with supplications; however, there are only a few of us willing to study God's Word as we should! Therefore, only a portion of God's armor is being used which means the believer is inept to war with the enemy on all fronts! This issue of only using a portion of God's armor is repeated many times over in the lives of Christians and it has weakened the church.

Be strong in the Lord and in the power of His might – As mentioned before, most of God's people are not being taught the full council of God's Word and the Word of the Kingdom which Jesus revealed to His followers. One of God's weapons against the wiles of Satan is to be strong in the Lord and in the power of His might. This is the manner of enduring human suffering! Scripture teaches us to understand that our strength lies in the endurance of afflictions and other type sufferings in the realization that the endurance is for Christ's sake. The Apostle Paul learned the dynamics of this revelation when a thorn was placed in his flesh by a messenger of Satan. Paul pleaded with the Lord three times to relieve him of this pain. The Lord responded in kind as follows:

"Concerning this thing I pleaded with the Lord three times that it might depart from me. And He said to me, "My grace is sufficient for you, for

My strength is made perfect in weakness." Therefore most gladly I will rather boast in my infirmities, that the power of Christ may rest upon me. Therefore I take pleasure in infirmities, in reproaches, in needs, in persecutions, in distresses, for Christ's sake. For when I am weak, then I am strong" 2 Corinthians 12:8-10 (NKJV).

The Scripture, "For when I am weak, then I am strong" provides a good spiritual example. Paul said, "For the weapons of our warfare are not carnal but mighty in God for pulling down strongholds" 2 Corinthians 10:4 (NKJV). He further stated, "Therefore I take pleasure in infirmities, in reproaches, in needs, in persecutions, in distresses, for Christ's sake. For when I am weak, then I am strong" 2 Corinthians 12:10 (NKJV). Paul told the Corinthians, "We are glad to seem weak if it helps show that you are actually strong. We pray that you will become mature" 2 Corinthians 13:9 (NLT). There are a multitude of Christians unaware that we must suffer for Christ and for ourselves. Now is the time for all Christians to become mature in the knowledge of Christ's suffering. "But rejoice to the extent that you partake of Christ's sufferings, that when His glory is revealed, you may also be glad with exceeding joy" 1 Peter 4:13 (NKJV). Paul advised the saints at Philippi, "Yet indeed I also count all things loss for the excellence of the knowledge of Christ Jesus my Lord, for whom I have suffered the loss of all things, and count them as rubbish, that I may gain Christ" Philippians 3:8 (NKJV). As faithful believers, we must not be ashamed of the Gospel. Paul revealed the reason to Timothy!

"Therefore do not be ashamed of the testimony of our Lord, nor of me His prisoner, but share with me in the sufferings for the gospel according to the power of God, who has saved us and called us with a holy calling, not according to our works, but according to His own purpose and grace which was given to us in Christ Jesus before time began, but has now been revealed by the appearing of our Savior Jesus Christ, who has abolished death and brought life and immortality to light through the gospel, to which I was appointed a preacher, an apostle, and a teacher of the Gentiles. For this reason I also suffer these things; nevertheless I am not ashamed, for I know whom I have believed

and am persuaded that He is able to keep what I have committed to Him until that Day" 2 Timothy 1:8-12 (NKJV).

Jesus teaches us through the Lord's Prayer to pray, "And do not lead us into temptation, But deliver us from the evil one" Matthew 6:13 (NKJV). Part of this temptation is the adversity, affliction, trouble sent by God to test our character, faith and holiness. Therefore, we must always remember that we should take pleasure in our weaknesses and in the insults, hardships, persecutions, and troubles as we suffer for Christ. For when we are weak, then we are strong in the Lord and in the power of His might.

Put on the whole armor of God that you may be able to stand against the wiles of the devil – Putting on the whole armor of God includes the shield, sword, lance, helmet, greaves, and breastplate. This is the way believers are able to stand against the wiles of Satan. The armor is the spiritual helps supplied by God for overcoming the temptations of the Devil. Satan's wiles are the cunning arts, deceit, craft and trickery he uses to deceive humans out of their inheritance. When the saints of God stand against the wiles of the devil, we grow in faith and knowledge of Jesus and mature in His likeness. "This will continue until we all come to such unity in our faith and knowledge of God's Son that we will be mature in the Lord, measuring up to the full and complete standard of Christ. Then we will no longer be immature like children. We won't be tossed and blown about by every wind of new teaching. We will not be influenced when people try to trick us with lies so clever they sound like the truth. Instead, we will speak the truth in love, growing in every way more and more like Christ, who is the head of his body, the church. He makes the whole body fit together perfectly. As each part does its own special work, it helps the other parts grow, so that the whole body is healthy and growing and full of love" Ephesians 4:13-16 (NLT).

For we do not wrestle against flesh and blood, but against principalities, against powers, against the rulers of the darkness of this age, against spiritual hosts of wickedness in the heavenly places – It is no secret that we live in a hard, cruel and perverse world. We know that the people of this world are not only cruel, but are selfish, demanding, vain, and only seem to care about themselves and those things which benefit them. They will do most anything to get their way including being hostile, abusive, cruel, vindictive and vengeful. This is the way of the world. Sadly enough, many these same attributes are being displayed by members in the household of faith. Many times these behaviors are demonstrated by someone close to us or even a family member. An example is when individuals show their ungodly and hateful ways. They display acts that are extremely hurtful, selfish and bitter; especially when the evilness or wicked behavior comes from a spouse, family member or someone we deeply trust! We have learned that the enemy's strategy is using others to do his dirty work; therefore we wrestle not against flesh and blood but against evil forces. It is still hard to focus on the *truth* rather than the perpetrators (people we know that are dear to us) of the situation.

Again, Scripture reveals to us that we do not wrestle against flesh and blood, but against principalities, against powers, against the rulers of the darkness of this age, against spiritual hosts of wickedness in the heavenly places. So what does this really mean? As we develop and mature in the things of the Lord, we must understand the truth and treat people accordingly by the Spirit. As believers, we can continue to blame the flesh of humans, such as our family, friends and other individuals for their actions and never move pass that level of growth. Now we must learn and understand that the warfare comes from the evil spirits within the person, not the individual! As knowledgeable Christians, we must understand how the enemy uses people and be able to pray for their deliverance. So many Christians become stagnant and crease to grow in the ways of God even though they may know God's Word. These things can grieve God's Spirit, because the Spirit leads and guides us in all truth so we can mature in wisdom and spiritual knowledge. Therefore, dealing with this situation with spiritual wisdom and knowledge helps us to unmask Satan and his angels!

The very first thing we must realize in all situations is the *weakness of the flesh*. The flesh denotes mere human nature; the earthly nature of man apart from divine influence is prone to sin and opposed to God. We pray that all believers are Spirit-filled and knowledgeable in things of the Lord, but that is not reality. All flesh is the same and have weaknesses;

some people's flesh is weaker than others. Some are being oppressed by satanic force and may need to overcome the bondage of this corrupt world. We may never know a person's situation, but we know Scripture and the truth; therefore, our maturity and wisdom in the Spirit may be all the Lord needs in a situation to restore others. We are called to help others, if we are mature enough to help according to the guidance of God's Spirit. "Brethren, if a man is overtaken in any trespass, you who are spiritual restore such a one in a spirit of gentleness, considering yourself lest you also be tempted" Galatians 6:1 (NKJV). Always remember, we are not dealing with flesh and blood, but in many cases we wrestle against unseen satanic powers that are influencing the other person.

Principalities are not always demonic in nature. They are sovereign, supreme powers; hence, superiority, predominance, high or the highest station. Therefore, some are holy angels used for the purposes of God. They can also be evil angels. They are fallen angels who are principalities and powers of Satan, the god of this world. They are beings that have and use power, influence, etc. in the unseen realms to oppose everything and everyone that is of God. Whatever power these evil forces possess, they are not beyond the control of our sovereign God, who uses even the wicked to bring about His perfect plan and purpose.

Rulers denote an authoritarian like-spirit of this world and ruler of darkness as define in the Blue Letter Bible. They are spirit powers, who, under the permissive will of God, and in consequence of human sin, exercise satanic powers and are therefore antagonistic authority over the world in its present condition of spiritual darkness and alienation from God. The rulers of darkness are defined as spiritual or moral darkness, emblematic of sin, as a condition of moral or spiritual depravity (an evil or immoral act). Metaphorically speaking, darkness is ignorance regarding divine things and human duties, and the accompanying ungodliness and immorality, together with a consequent misery in a burning hell. The spiritual hosts or ruler of this world is the lord of this world, the prince of this age, Satan, the devil and his demons. These evil beings influence spiritual wickedness in the people of the earth in the form of malice, depravity, iniquity, wickedness, evil purposes and evil desires. They lie and wait in the sphere of activity or existence which is far above in heavenly places in contrast to the earth. They are known as principalities, powers, and spiritual hosts of wickedness that operate in those individuals who live according to the flesh!

Therefore take up the whole armor of God that you may be able to withstand in the evil day, and having done all, to stand – To *take up* is to lay hold of. It is to take up, to carry and/or use it. The full armor includes the shield, sword, lance, helmet, greaves, and breastplate. Metaphorically, taking of the full armor of God is presenting the members of the body as instruments of *righteousness* instead of presenting them as instruments of *unrighteousness* as revealed in Romans 6:12-14 (NKJV) – "Therefore do not let sin reign in your mortal body, that you should obey it in its lusts. And do not present your members as instruments of unrighteousness to sin, but present yourselves to God as being alive from the dead, and your members as instruments of righteousness to God. For sin shall not have dominion over you, for you are not under law but *under grace*."

God's armor is of the spiritual helps supplied by Him for overcoming the temptations of the devil. It is also to arm you with the same mind as that of Christ in regard to His sufferings. Those who are suffering physically for Christ have finished with sin. "So then, since Christ suffered physical pain, you must arm yourselves with the same attitude he had, and be ready to suffer, too. For if you have suffered physically for Christ, you have finished with sin. You won't spend the rest of your lives chasing your own desires, but you will be anxious to do the will of God" 1 Peter 4:1-2 (NLT).

Being able to *withstand* is having the power to resist evil forces whether by virtue of one's own ability and resources or state of mind, or through favorable circumstances, or by permission of law or custom. It denotes the ability, force, and strength that God bestows upon believers through His Spirit. The phrase, *the power of His might* indicates strength afforded from God's power by His Spirit. The glory of His might signifies the visible expression of the inherent personal power of the Lord Jesus.

To stand is the ability to set one's self against, to withstand, resist and oppose such as God's armor enables the believer to resist the devil.

"Therefore submit to God. Resist the devil and he will flee from you" James 4:7 (NKJV). In that day is *any day* one experiences oppression. Like the days of bringing toils, annoyances, perils; it's a time full of peril in Christian faith and steadfastness that causes pain and trouble. That evil day is when evil will cause labor, pain, sorrow, malignant evil, disease or blindness.

Remember, God's armor is the spiritual helps supplied by Him for overcoming the temptations of the devil; to stand means to continue to be safe and sound, unharmed and ready. To be of a steadfast mind and of quality, of one who does not hesitate or does not waiver. God's armor enables the believer to resist the devil and his temptations, to have that state of mind to endure the days that Satan brings toils, annoyances, and perils. For in those evil days he causes labor, pain, sorrow, malignant evil, disease or blindness to Christians who are weak in faith and do not use the armor of God as it was intended! God has given us the ability to remain steadfast while presenting the members of our bodies as instruments of righteousness instead of spending the rest of our lives chasing our own fleshly desires.

Stand therefore, having girded your waist with truth – We live in a time and stage of life where many rebellious leaders in the Christian community is engaging in unessential and useless ministry and is deceiving many congregants. Peter spoke of the destructive doctrine with which our generation would be confronted. He said in 2 Peter 2:1 (NLT) – "But there were also false prophets in Israel, just as there will be false teachers among you. They will cleverly teach destructive heresies and even deny the Master who bought them. In this way, they will bring sudden destruction on themselves." Therefore, the truth of God's Word will be abated (become weaker and decrease in strength). Jesus confronted the scribes and the Pharisees with Isaiah's prophesy that also spoke to this very issue. He said, "Hypocrites! Well did Isaiah prophesy about you, saying: 'These people draw near to Me with their mouth, and honor Me with their lips, but their heart is far from Me. And in vain they worship Me, teaching as doctrines the commandments of men" Matthew 15:7-9 (NKJV).

I cannot over emphasize the important of studying God's Word! I am reminded of Jesus words. One of His many phrases was, "And you shall know the truth, and the truth shall make you free" John 8:32 (NKJV). In order to withstand Satan and his forces, one must know the truth. An important ingredient of God's armor is having girded your waist with truth. This means to stand your ground; put on the belt of truth and the body armor of God's righteousness. In other words, believers must equip themselves with knowledge of the truth. The truth I speak of is the truth as taught in the Christian religion, respecting God and the execution of his purposes through Christ, and respecting the duties of man. Also, one must oppose the superstitions of weak believers, the inventions of the Jews, and the corrupt opinions and precepts of false teachers.

Metaphorically speaking, girding your loins with truth is bracing yourself to maintain perfect sincerity and reality as counteractive forces in Christian character against hypocrisy and falsehood. Today's church world has a habit of listening to a pastor for truth and not validating and/or qualifying the pastor's words with their own study. This scenario means that the believer's salvation is totally dependent upon the wisdom and spiritual knowledge of the pastor/minister.

Many times a situation develops where the blind is leading the blind. Jesus' disciples inquired of Him about His words to the Pharisees when the Pharisees became offended. "But He answered and said, "Every plant [God's servants] which My heavenly Father has not planted will be uprooted. Let them alone. They are blind leaders of the blind. And if the blind leads the blind, both will fall into a ditch" Matthew 15:13-14 (NKJV). Everyone's spiritual growth and development, hence salvation, rest totally with the believer. God will judge all ministers and spiritual teachers in association with their calling and responsibility. Those who defile the temples of the Holy Spirit (spirit-filled believers) with be destroyed. "If anyone defiles the temple of God, God will destroy him. For the temple of God is holy, which temple you are" 1 Corinthians 3:17 (NKJV).

Put on the breastplate of righteousness - A breastplate or corset consist of two parts that protects the body on both sides from the neck to the middle. The breastplate speaks metaphorically of righteousness. "Stand your ground, putting on the belt of truth and the body armor of God's righteousness" Ephesians 6:14 (NLT). It also speaks of faith and love.

"But let us who live in the light be clearheaded, protected by the armor of faith and love, and wearing as our helmet the confidence of our salvation" 1 Thessalonians 5:8 (NLT).

Shod your feet with the preparation of the gospel of peace – To shod your feet is to bind yourself with spiritual readiness. Bind means to make or become fast or secure; to place oneself under obligation. Therefore, it is having the feet shod (bond, ready, prepared) with the preparation of the Gospel of peace. The Gospel itself is the firm footing of the believer, his/her walk being worthy of it and therefore a testimony in regard to it. The Gospel of peace is of Christianity, the tranquil state of a soul assured of its salvation through Christ, and so fearing nothing from God and content with its earthly lot, of whatsoever sort that is. It is the blessed state of devout and upright men and women after death. After death can be a physical death or the *life* of a born-again Christian that lives according to God's Spirit and not according to their flesh which brings death. "For if you live according to the flesh you will die; but if by the Spirit you put to death the deeds of the body, you will live" Romans 8:13 (NKJV).

Above all, take the shield of faith to quench all the fiery darts of the wicked one - A shield is a broad piece of armor made of rigid material and strapped to the arm or carried in the hand for protection against hurled or thrusted weapons which protects every part of a soldier. The word is used meta-phorically of *faith* in this Scripture which the believer is to take up which affects the soldier's activities. Faith is the conviction that God exists and is the creator and ruler of all things, and that He is the provider and the one who bestows eternal salvation through Jesus Christ. We all know that, "Faith is the substance of things hoped for, the evidence of things not seen" Hebrews 11:1 (NKJV).

Through faith, the believer is able to extinguish, quench, suppress or stifle the fiery darts of the enemy. Fiery darts of the enemy are destructive guided projectiles which cause sudden pain and/or distress in the lives of God's people. They are designed to bring toils, annoyances and perils to the Christian faith and steadfastness; they cause pain and trouble. Satan's fiery darts are destructive projectiles delivered to change a believer's way of thinking, feeling and acting, along with their thoughts and desires. But God is faithful and has given us spiritual weapons to stand against all of the wiles of Satan. However, we must put on the full armor of God which includes the shield, sword, lance, helmet, greaves, and breastplate. This is the way we believers are able to stand against the wiles of Satan and his fiery darts.

And take the helmet of salvation, and the sword of the Spirit, which is the word of God - The helmet is various protective head coverings usually made of a hard material to resist impact. Metaphorically it is the protection of the soul which consists in (the hope of) salvation. Now salvation is an experience of the Lord's deliverance of believers, as of those who are engaged in spiritual conflict. The sword, on the other hand, is metaphorically the Word of God; the sword of the Spirit probes the believer's conscience and subdues the believer's impulses to sin.

As believers, we must understand God's purpose in humankind. Even though we sin and fall short of His glory and live under His curse which gives authority to Satan to bruise the heel (alter our steps) of God's people, we have been given spiritual weapons and power by God's Spirit to endure and overcome the wiles (Satan's cunning arts, deceit, craft and trickery) of the enemy! Enduring is to carry on despite hardships and suffering. Overcoming is to successfully deal with or gain control of (something difficult). Therefore, realizing that we will encounter tribulations, afflictions, trials, hardships and suffering, we can still triumph over despair and troubles through the faith that God gives each one who belongs to His Son, Jesus Christ. Furthermore, we know these tribulations are designed to produce perseverance, character and hope. "Therefore, having been justified by faith, we have peace with God through our Lord Jesus Christ, through whom also we have access by faith into this grace in which we stand, and rejoice in hope of the glory of God. And not only that, but we also glory in tribulations, knowing that tribulation produces perseverance; and perseverance, character; and character, hope. Now hope does not disappoint, because the love of God has been poured out in our hearts by the Holy Spirit who was given to us" Romans 5:1-5 (NKJV).

Praying always with all prayer and supplication in the Spirit, being watchful to this end with all perseverance and supplication for all the saints – The most essential undertaking a believer can do is maintain a life with God by offering all prayers and supplication in the Spirit to Him. "But you, beloved, building yourselves up on your most holy faith, praying in the Holy Spirit, keep yourselves in the love of God, looking for the mercy of our Lord Jesus Christ unto eternal life. And on some have compassion, making a distinction" Jude 1:20-22 (NKJV). Supplication is the act of communicating with a deity as in a petition or in adoration or contrition (sincere remorse for wrongdoing; repentance) or thanksgiving. It is a seeking, asking, and entreating God.

We already know we are sinful creatures living in this weak flesh; however, God's Spirit helps us in our weakness and makes intercession for us according to *His will.* "Likewise the Spirit also helps in our weaknesses. For we do not know what we should pray for as we ought, but the Spirit Himself makes intercession for us with groanings which cannot be uttered. Now He who searches the hearts knows what the mind of the Spirit is, because He makes intercession for the saints according to the will of God." Romans 8:26-27 (NKJV).

As believers, sometimes we do not know what to pray for; especially when it comes to lining our prayers up with God's will and His holy Word. Therefore, when the believer prays in the Sprit, as stated above in Romans 8:26-27, God's Spirit helps in our weaknesses by making intercession for us with groanings which cannot be uttered. "For he that speaks in an unknown tongue speaks not unto men, but unto God: for no man understands him; howbeit in the spirit he speaks mysteries" 1 Corinthians 14:2 (KJV). The mysteries are a hidden or secret thing, not obvious to the understanding. The mysteries are a hidden purpose or counsel of God which is secret. It's how God governs his dealings with the righteous while keeping the secrets hidden from ungodly and wicked men. It is important to pray to God and to pray in the Spirit. James advised us to "Confess your faults one to another, and pray one for another, that ye may be healed. The effectual fervent prayer of a righteous man avails much" James 5:16 (KJV). In reading this Scripture, we realize that the earnest prayer of a righteous person has great power and produces wonderful results. But, *do not be deceived*, the Scripture clearly reveals it is the fervent prayer of *righteous individuals* that avails much.

The word righteous means one who is righteous, observing divine laws. It is one who is upright, innocent, faultless, guiltless, and virtuous and keeps the commands of God. A righteous person is one whose way of thinking, feeling, and acting is wholly conformed to the will of God, and who therefore needs no rectification(To set right; correct) in the heart or life. The paradigm (a theory or a group of ideas about how something should be done, made, or thought) of many Christians believes that anyone can pray and their prayers will avail much. In other words, they believe their prayers have great power and will produce many wonderful results. All they have to do is pray! However, *this type thinking does not line up with the Word of God.* Clearly, it is the prayers of a righteous man and women, who needs no rectification, has great power and produces wonderful results. As Jesus said when He spoke to His disciples, "And Jesus answered and said to them: "Take heed that *no one deceives you*. For many will come in My name, saying, 'I am the Christ,' and *will deceive many*" Matthew 24:4-5 (NKJV). Because there are many false leaders in today's churches, many will be deceived.

USE GOD'S WEAPONS OR CONTINUE TO OPERATE IN THE NATURAL WITHOUT POWER!

As you can see, God has given His people many weapons to battle unseen and evil spiritual forces. These weapons provide human flesh the ability to rely on God's powers to battle our enemies, whoever they may be! Even though we are cast down, we are not conquered. We now have this light shining in our hearts, but we ourselves are like fragile clay jars containing this great treasure. This makes it clear that our great power is from God, *not from ourselves*. I get so tired of church leaders taking credit for God's anointing power in healing or blessing saints of God. Sometime they say, "I prayed for this person and they got healed as if the person's healing was dependent upon their prayers. God uses His servants as conduits to bless His people, but make no mistake that the power comes from Him and Him only!

"We are pressed on every side by troubles, but we are not crushed. We are perplexed, but not driven to despair. We are hunted down, but never abandoned by God. We get knocked down, but we are not destroyed. Through suffering, our bodies continue to share in the death of Jesus so that the life of Jesus may also be seen in our bodies" 2 Corinthians 4:7-10 (NLT). "That is why we never give up. Though our bodies are dying, our spirits are being renewed every day. For our present troubles are small and won't last very long. Yet they produce for us a glory that vastly outweighs them and will last forever! So we don't look at the troubles we can see now; rather, we fix our gaze on things that cannot be seen. For the things we see now will soon be gone, but the things we cannot see will last forever" 2 Corinthians 4:16-18 (NLT).

How good would a military unit be that does not use its weapons to defend and overcome its enemies? They would not be good at all! What if an Army that has been allocated armor, weapons and a plan of defense against its enemies is suddenly, in the middle of the battle, no longer *empowered* to use their armament? The army would no longer have the ability to finish their assignment and do the things they were appointed (called) to do! The same scenario applies to believers in the body of Christ. Christians are soldiers in God's army predestined and called to perform a Divine assignment while on this earth. Even though humans became weakened vessels because of disobedience, God made provisions before the world was formed for all humanity to be redeemed through the blood of Jesus Christ. He allocated power from on high to not only battle the forces of evil, but to endure and overcome them with the weapons of warfare He provides. When we unite with Christ, we receive an inheritance from God; for He chose us in advance and he makes everything work out according to his plan. This plan is achieved when you become a child of God through the power and guidance of His Spirit!

Chapter five reveals the awesome power believers receive to battle unseen forces in the spirit world. Humans must clearly learn and understand that only *faithful believers* are able to live according to God's Spirit and be freed from the law of sin and death. Believers must be obedient to God's Word in order to become righteous beings and to be pleasing to Him as recorded by the apostle Paul in Romans. "For the law of the Spirit of life in Christ Jesus has made me free from the law of sin and death. For what the law could not do in that it was weak through the flesh, God did by sending His own Son in the likeness of sinful flesh, on account of sin: He condemned sin in the flesh, that the righteous requirement of the law might be fulfilled in us who do not walk according to the flesh but according to the Spirit" Romans 8:2-4 (NKJV).

Furthermore, "Because the carnal mind is enmity against God; for it is not subject to the law of God, nor indeed can be. So then, those who are in the flesh cannot please God" Romans 8:7-8 (NKJV) and "If you live according to the flesh you will die; but if by the Spirit you put to death the deeds of the body, you will live. For as many as are led by the Spirit of God, these are sons of God" Romans 8:13-14 (NKJV). Please pray before you read the next chapter that you will receive understanding by God's Spirit because the chapter _only_ gives spiritual insight. If the revelation in this chapter seems strange to you or is foolishness to you, I am afraid you are still operating according to the carnal mind and living by the flesh as revealed in 1 Corinthians 2:14 (NKJV) – "But the natural man does not receive the things of the Spirit of God, for they are foolishness to him; nor can he know them, because they are spiritually discerned." Hopefully, you will have eyes to see by the Spirit!

CHAPTER 5

Not by Might, Power or Our Flesh, but by God's Spirit!

HUMAN FLESH IS INCAPABLE OF PULLING DOWN SPIRITUAL STRONGHOLDS!

As REVEALED IN THE LAST chapter, because of God's curse, humans were made to encounter a hostile and adversarial world that brought forth tribulations, sorrows, afflictions and spiritual warfare to God's people. These adversities would occur in all of the human life on earth. However, God did not leave us without hope! In the fullness of God's time, He gave the world His Son, Jesus Christ and His Spirit. Believing Christians are now able to endure and overcome the wiles of Satan. The power of God's Spirit in human flesh has the ability to pull down spiritual strong holds through the spiritual weapons God has given to those who believe. These weapons are birthed in those who love the Lord and live according to the ways of God's Spirit. This way, the saints of God live in human flesh but not war according to the flesh. "For though we walk in the flesh, we do not war according to the flesh. Human flesh is in capable of spiritual warfare. As revealed, the weapons of warfare come to us by God's Spirit.

The Kingdom of God assuredly suffers violence from the enemies of God. Many of these enemies are in human flesh because they have given themselves over to the god of this world. Yet, as faithful believers we press through the opposition of the enemy by the power of God's Spirit to obtain citizenship in the Kingdom of God. As Christians, we have to fight through circumstance of tribulation, hardships, afflictions and oppression from God's adversaries. Many times our opposition is not only from those in the world, but also from those in the household of faith.

Malicious opposition many times come from religious leaders, like John the Baptist experienced. He received strong opposition from the Pharisees and the Sadducees because they rejected Jesus Christ and the word of the Kingdom. The Jewish nation of that day simply did not address leaders, religious or otherwise for fear of punishment. However, John's faith made him fearless in the face of opposition.

This chapter is a reminder that God's power is *only* entrusted to those who believe in Jesus Christ, who maintain their love, faith and obedience in Him. Many individuals initially believe in Jesus and are endowed with God's Spirit at rebirth. However, due to the lust and desires of their flesh, they give way to ungodly behaviors. This is the nature of this world and its god, Satan! The world only offers us a craving for physical pleasure and pride in achievements and possessions. "For all that is in the world—the lust of the flesh, the lust of the eyes, and the pride of life—is not of the Father but is of the world" 1 John 2:16 (NKJV). It is amazing how many Christians crave and seek the things of this world as if this world is eternal and their earthly achievements are the main ingredients of this life! Yes, I say Christians because so many are deceived into lusting after wealth, popularity, unnatural sexual behaviors, controls and much more! Instead of seeking God's Kingdom, many seek the things of this world. However, this is neither our world nor the life we should be seeking! Many of God's people have their eyes set on the wrong things. Jesus said, "But seek first the kingdom of God and His righteousness, and all these things shall be added to you" Matthew 6:33 (NKJV).

There are so many Christians who are unaware of the methodology of receiving and maintaining the Holy Spirit which grant unto believers spiritual power to battle the forces of evil. Individuals receive the indwelling of God's Spirit when they believe in Jesus Christ. I realize that many believe there must be a laying on of hands or someone speaking in tongues for believers to receive the Holy Spirit. These events occurred in many of the impartations of God's Spirit in certain situations in the New Testament period, and many of today's ministers still use this process to indwell the believer with God's Spirit. However, it is not necessary because God's people receive His Spirit at the rebirth. Being *born-again* is of God making believers His sons/daughters through faith in Christ's work. As quoted from the Blue Letter Bible - Apostle John's definition of the rebirth is: of the gracious act of God in conferring upon those who believe the nature and disposition of "children," imparting to them spiritual life. The Scripture in Ephesians reveals the truth of God's people receiving the Holy Spirit. "In Him you also trusted, after you heard the word of truth, the gospel of your salvation; in whom also, *having believed*, you were *sealed* with the Holy Spirit of promise, who is the guarantee of our inheritance until the redemption of the purchased possession, to the praise of His glory" Ephesians 1:13-14 (NKJV).

Being sealed is a spiritual process which occurs in the believer to prove, confirm, or attest them before God. It means ownership and security, together with destination. As mentioned before, the metaphor of *sealing of believers* occurs by the gift of the Holy Spirit, upon believing souls at the time of their regeneration, not after a lapse of time in their spiritual life. Those individuals sealed are being secured from destruction and marked for reward. Security from destruction and the receipt of rewards is totally dependent upon the believer *maintaining their spiritual life* according to the word of God. I repeat: Believers must maintain their spiritual life in order for the Holy Spirit to remain active and effective.

A multitude of Christians seem *confused* on the matter of sinning because many of them think God's grace overrides their infidelity, greed, fornication, idolatry, selfish ambitions and the like. Obedience was required in the Garden of Eden, throughout the Old and the New Testament periods, as well as, on the earth today! God may give us a period of time to correct our behavior as the Holy Spirit attempts to teach us truth; however, that widow closes at the point of death. Whatever we are when death comes to us is the way we will be judged. At that point, there is no turning or excuses for what was done and what should have happen. Christian believers are expected to learn God's will, develop and mature in the knowledge of truth and allow this truth to be reflective in their lives. This is the reason God gives us His Spirit! His Spirit not only comforts believers in their time of dismay but the Spirit also leads and guides God's people in all truth when they seek God's Kingdom.

Even in the ministry of today's churches, I find Christians who still *do not* understand the quintessential need for the indwelling and maintaining of God's Spirit. Many believers understand the Holy Spirit is the Spirit of truth and that He indwells the believer. However, not all understand that the filling of the Spirit is a repeated experience. There are many believers who do not understand that they can quench the Holy Spirit and cause Him to be ineffective in their lives. Furthermore, there is a multitude of Christians who do not understand that if the Spirit is *not active* in a believer's life, it is impossible to *please* God nor will that person receive the inheritance promised to all believers! Perhaps the next segment might enlighten those who are unaware of the quintessential needs to live according to God's Spirit.

The following two Scripture are extremely important for a believer to learn, understand and live by. They provide a small, but important revelation of how God foreknew the weakness of humans and that humans would initially fail to be obedient to His Word in the Garden of Eden. The Scriptures also demonstrate that God always had a plan for our redemption!

"Blessed be the God and Father of our Lord Jesus Christ, who has blessed us with every spiritual blessing in the heavenly places in Christ, just as He chose us in Him before the foundation of the world, that we should be holy and without blame before Him in love, having predestined us to adoption as sons by Jesus Christ to Himself, according to the good pleasure of His will, to the praise of the glory of His grace, by which He made us accepted in the Beloved" Ephesians 1:3-6 (NKJV).

"And we know that all things work together for good to those who love God, to those who are the called according to His purpose. For whom He foreknew, He also predestined to be conformed to the image of His Son, that He might be the firstborn among many brethren. Moreover whom He predestined, these He also called; whom He called, these He also justified; and whom He justified, and these He also glorified" Romans 8:28-30 (NKJV).

There are no accidents in God and in His creation. God has always had a plan that included Jesus Christ, Satan's oppression and the Holy Spirit. It also included the deliverance of those who love Jesus, those who have faith in Him and those who obey His Word.

ETERNAL LIFE IS ONLY ACHIEVED THROUGH BELIEF IN JESUS AND LIVING ACCORDING TO THE HOLY SPIRIT!

Christians everywhere know and understand that salvation comes by believing in Jesus Christ. However, as mentioned above, few understand that it is God's Spirit that provides the weapons and power to endure and overcome the wiles of Satan. Furthermore, if you quench the Spirit during your life and do not repent and ask the Lord for forgiveness of your unrighteousness, you will not be saved! *Hear me clearly!* As believers, we receive the Holy Spirit at the time of our conversion. We become the temples of God's Spirit bought with a price and no longer belong to ourselves but belong to God. "Or do you not know that your body is the temple of the Holy Spirit who is in you, whom you have from God, and you are not your own? For you were bought at a price; therefore glorify God in your body and in your spirit, which are God's" 1 Corinthians 6:19-20 (NKJV). For this reason, we must glorify God in our bodies and in our spirts by glorifying Him in our thoughts or with the heart. Also, by acknowledging His excellence and rendering homage to; to magnify Him in worship and to adore Him. Believers vindicate God's glory by our actions, deeds and the things we do.

As we live according to God's Spirit, we become a witness in the Kingdom of God because the Holy Spirit gives power to true believers. Here's a fallacy: Almost every Christian believes they are indwelled by the Holy Spirit and live by Him! This is not true because many have quenched the Spirit perhaps unknowingly. It is so easy to say "I believe in Jesus and have faith in Him," but in reality, your works do not support your witness. The statement, *faith without works is dead* is true as per the following Scripture!

"What good is it, dear brothers and sisters, if you say you have faith but don't show it by your actions? Can that kind of faith save anyone? Suppose you see a

brother or sister who has no food or clothing, and you say, "Good-bye and have a good day; stay warm and eat well"—but then you don't give that person any food or clothing. What good does that do? So you see, faith by itself isn't enough. Unless it produces good deeds, it is dead and useless.

Now someone may argue, "Some people have faith; others have good deeds." But I say, "How can you show me your faith if you don't have good deeds? I will show you my faith by my good deeds." You say you have faith, for you believe that there is one God. Good for you! Even the demons believe this, and they tremble in terror. How foolish! Can't you see that faith without good deeds is useless?

Don't you remember that our ancestor Abraham was shown to be right with God by his actions when he offered his son Isaac on the altar? You see his faith and his actions worked together. His actions made his faith complete. And so it happened just as the Scriptures say: "Abraham believed God, and God counted him as righteous because of his faith." He was even called the friend of God. So you see we are shown to be right with God by what we do, not by faith alone" James 2:14-24 (NLT).

If someone is indwelled with the Holy Spirit, they know that faith without works is dead and that they can produce works and deeds to prove faith. These are the individuals who seek God's Kingdom and the power of His Spirit. They are found holy and worthy before Him. They also seek God to be free of indwelling sin. God's Spirit gives us _power_ to pull down spiritual strongholds, freedom from indwelling sin, freedom from the law of sin and death, and to become the sons and daughters of God. As long as the believer continues to live according to God's Spirit, they maintain their _eternal_ inheritance and _life_ in the Kingdom of God. The Holy Spirit, the Divine energy of God helps the believer to fulfill the divine calling of God and to carry out the work God has called him or her to do.

As believers, we must understand that spiritual growth, worthy accomplishments, wisdom, ability to resist, knowledge, righteousness, love, faith, obedience and more indwells human flesh by God's Spirit. Everything we do, possess, experience, knows and more comes from God. Human flesh has a tendency to believe that we have the power to overcome circumstances in life and that we can rebuke and bind Satan as we choose. This way of thinking is the deception from our enemy. We are *totally dependent* on God for everything good in our lives. This is why humans cannot continue to exist on the earth without the indwelling power of God's Spirit. I believe our evilness would completely destroy us without God's Spirit! In little or no time, we would turn on each other and eradicate one another in our attempt to be the number one person in charge! See below the impact of life without God's Spirit.

Then the LORD God took the man and put him in the Garden of Eden to tend and keep it. And the LORD God commanded the man, saying, "Of every tree of the garden you may freely eat; but of the tree of the knowledge of good and evil you shall not eat, for in the day that you eat of it you shall surely die" Genesis 2:15-17 (NKJV). The death that man endured was spiritual death. God separated Himself from man which meant that God removed His Spirit from the life of man on the earth! Therefore, humankind no longer had *spiritual guidance* except in those situations where God visited man for a Divine purpose. As mentioned, God foreknew our weakness and disobedience; therefore, He predestined Jesus Christ as Savior and returned His Spirit to indwell human flesh for order, design, love, faith and obedience. In other words, life itself comes to human flesh only through Jesus Christ and by God's Spirit. Everything from God is made available by His Spirit.

"So he answered and said to me: "This is the word of the LORD to Zerubbabel: 'Not by might nor by power, but by My Spirit,' Says the LORD of hosts" Zechariah 4:6 (NKJV). The word *might* means strength, efficiency, wealth or by an army. The definition of *power* is human strength, strength, produce, wealth (of soil). The Spirit is Spirit of God, the third person of the triune God, the Holy Spirit, coequal, coeternal with the Father and the Son.

Consequently, those who walk and live according to their flesh *do not* please God. However, those who walk and live according to the *Spirit* are *pleasing* to God. The only way to be righteous before God is when the Holy Spirit continues to *fill* faithful believers with God's power from on high. Whenever we sin, four actions have to take place: 1) we must recognize the sin; 2) we must ask Jesus for forgiveness of our sins with a contrite heart; 3) we must ask for the refilling of the Holy Spirit: and 4) we must turn away from the sin. This is known as refilling of the Holy Spirit which is different from the initial indwelling of the Spirit. God's Spirit is able to do the following in human flesh:

- *Provides freedom from condemnation* – "There is therefore now no condemnation to those who are in Christ Jesus, who do not walk according to the flesh, but according to the Spirit" Romans 8:1 (NKJV).
- *Gives freedom from the law of sin and death* - "For what the law could not do in that it was weak through the flesh, God did by sending His own Son in the likeness of sinful flesh, on account of sin: He condemned sin in the flesh, that the righteous requirement of the law might be fulfilled in us who do not walk according to the flesh but according to the Spirit" Romans 8:3-4 (NKJV).
- *Replaces the carnal mind* – "For those who live according to the flesh set their minds on the things of the flesh, but those who live according to the Spirit, the things of the Spirit. For to be carnally minded is death, but to be spiritually minded is life and peace. Because the carnal mind is enmity against God; for it is not subject to the law of God, nor indeed can be. So then, those who are in the flesh cannot please God" Romans 8:5-8 (NKJV).
- *Gives life to the mortal body* – "But you are not in the flesh but in the Spirit, if indeed the Spirit of God dwells in you. Now if anyone does not have the Spirit of Christ, he is not His. And if Christ *is* in you, the body *is* dead because of sin, but the Spirit *is* life because of righteousness. But if the Spirit of Him who raised Jesus from the dead dwells in you, He who raised Christ from the dead will also give life to your mortal bodies through His Spirit who dwells in you" Romans 8:9-11 (NKJV).
- *Puts to death the deeds of their flesh and makes you sons and/or daughters of God* – "For if you live according to the flesh you will die; but if by the Spirit you put to death the deeds of the body, you will live.

For as many as are led by the Spirit of God, these are sons of God" Romans 8:13-14 (NKJV).

- *Gives power to resist the devil and cause him to flee* – "Therefore submit to God. Resist the devil and he will flee from you" James 4:7 (NKJV).

- *Provides weapons of warfare* – "For the weapons of our warfare are not carnal but mighty in God for pulling down strongholds, casting down arguments and every high thing that exalts itself against the knowledge of God, bringing every thought into captivity to the obedience of Christ, and being ready to punish all disobedience when your obedience is fulfilled" 2 Corinthians 10:4-6 (NKJV).

- *Helps you stand against the wiles of Satan* - "Finally, my brethren, be strong in the Lord and in the power of His might. Put on the whole armor of God that you may be able to stand against the wiles of the devil. For we do not wrestle against flesh and blood, but against principalities, against powers, against the rulers of the darkness of this age, against spiritual hosts of wickedness in the heavenly places. Therefore take up the whole armor of God, that you may be able to withstand in the evil day, and having done all, to stand.

  Stand therefore, having girded your waist with truth, having put on the breastplate of righteousness, and having shod your feet with the preparation of the gospel of peace; above all, taking the shield of faith with which you will be able to quench all the fiery darts of the wicked one. And take the helmet of salvation, and the sword of the Spirit, which is the word of God; praying always with all prayer and supplication in the Spirit, being watchful to this end with all perseverance and supplication for all the saints" Ephesians 6:10-18 (NKJV).

- *Gives the believer power to resist the temptations of Satan* - "Then Jesus was led up by the Spirit into the wilderness to be tempted by the devil. And when He had fasted forty days and forty nights, afterward He was hungry. Now when the tempter came to Him, he said, "If You are the Son of God, command that these stones become bread." But He answered and said, "It is written, 'Man shall not live by bread alone, but by every word that proceeds from the mouth of God.'

Then the devil took Him up into the holy city, set Him on the pinnacle of the temple, and said to Him, "If You are the Son of God, throw Yourself down. For it is written: 'He shall give His angels charge over you 'and, 'in their hands they shall bear you up, lest you dash your foot against a stone.' Jesus said to him, "It is written again, 'You shall not tempt the LORD your God.'"

Again, the devil took Him up on an exceedingly high mountain, and showed Him all the kingdoms of the world and their glory. And he said to Him, "All these things I will give you if you will fall down and worship me." Then Jesus said to him, "Away with you, Satan! For it is written, 'You shall worship the LORD your God, and Him only you shall serve.'" Then the devil left Him, and behold, angels came and ministered to Him" Matthew 4:1-11 (NKJV).

- *Produces the fruit of the Spirit* – "But the fruit of the Spirit is love, joy, peace, longsuffering, kindness, goodness, faithfulness, gentleness, self-control. Against such there is no law" Galatians 5:22-23 (NKJV).

- *Gives you power to live according to the rules of the Kingdom* – "But I say to you who hear: Love your enemies, do good to those who hate you, bless those who curse you, and pray for those who spitefully use you. To him who strikes you on the one cheek, offer the other also. And from him, who takes away your cloak, do not withhold your tunic either. Give to everyone who asks of you. And from him who takes away your goods do not ask them back. And just as you want men to do to you, you also do to them likewise.

"But if you love those who love you, what credit is that to you? For even sinners love those who love them. And if you do good to those who do good to you, what credit is that to you? For even sinners do the same. And if you lend to those from whom you hope to receive back, what credit is that to you? For even sinners lend to sinners to receive as much back. But love your enemies, do good, and lend, hoping for nothing in return; and your reward will be great, and you will be sons of the Most High. For He is kind to the unthankful and evil. Therefore be merciful, just as your Father also is merciful.

"Judge not, and you shall not be judged. Condemn not, and you shall not be condemned. Forgive, and you will be forgiven. Give and it will be given to you: good measure, pressed down, shaken together, and running over will be put into your bosom. For with the same measure that you use, it will be measured back to you" Luke 6:27-38 (NKJV).

- *Helps you restore others* – "Brethren, if a man is overtaken in any trespass, you who are *spiritual* restore such a one in a spirit of gentleness, considering yourself lest you also be tempted" Galatians 6:1 (NKJV).

- *Gives you power to endure to the end* – God's Spirit gives the believer power to endure and overcome the adversities of life. In the last days, many will suffer persecutions. "Yes, and all who desire to live godly in Christ Jesus will suffer persecution" 2 Timothy 3:12 (NKJV). However, Jesus prophesied the last days for our awareness and for believers to remain strong and not fear. He advised us not to be deceived and to endure to the end. "But he who endures to the end shall be saved" Matthew 24:13 (NKJV).

- *Convicts the world* – "Nevertheless I [Jesus] tell you the truth. It is to your advantage that I go away; for if I do not go away, the Helper [Holy Spirit] will not come to you; but if I depart, I will send Him to you. And when He has come, He will convict the world of sin, and of righteousness, and of judgment: of sin, because they do not believe in Me; of righteousness, because I go to My Father and you see Me no more; of judgment, because the ruler of this world is judged" John 16:7-11 (NKJV).

Finally, the indwelling of God's Spirit and being constantly filled by the Spirit *enables* you to achieve *eternal life*. The *only* way to salvation is through the blood of Jesus *and* living according to God's Spirit. **Yes, you must not only believe in Jesus, but you must also *live according* to God's Spirit.** Spirit-filled believers are temples of the Holy Spirit. When you first believed in Jesus, you were sealed by God as His! The seal of the living God is an emblem of ownership and security. God's Spirit seals you and makes you secures you from destruction and marks you for reward. Once sealed by God, you are not your own and therefore you belong to God who bought you at a price. "Run from sexual sin! No other sin as clearly affects the body as this one does. For sexual immorality is a sin against your own body. Don't you realize that your body is the temple of the Holy Spirit, who lives in you and was given to you by God? You do not belong to yourself, for God bought you with a high price. So you must honor God with your body" 1 Corinthians 6:18-20 (NLT). This revelation should be taught again and again because so many get involved in sexual sins.

Just know that God's anger will come upon those who disobey our Lord Jesus in His Gospel. "For the wrath of God is revealed from heaven against all ungodliness and unrighteousness of men, who suppress the truth in unrighteousness" Romans 1:18 (NKJV). Believers must repent and turn away from all unrighteousness! "Because you are not sorry for your sins and will not turn from them, you will be punished even more on the day of God's anger. God will be right in saying you are guilty. He will give to every man what he should get for the things he has done. Those who keep on doing good and are looking for His greatness and honor will receive life that lasts forever. Those who love only themselves and do not obey the truth, but do what is wrong, will be punished by God. His anger will be upon them. Every person, whether Jew or not, who is a sinner will suffer and have great sorrow. But God will give His greatness and honor and peace to all those who obey the truth. Both Jews and those who are not Jews will receive this" Romans 2:5-10 (NLV). Only those who were Spirit-filled were gathered into the wedding feast, both good and bad. The truth of this revelation is clearly demonstrated in Jesus' parable of the ten virgins.

REVELATION OF THOSE WHO WILL INHERIT ETERNAL LIFE!

Jesus told His disciples that His followers (the multitude) had not been given to know the mysteries of the Kingdom. It is interesting to know that only disciples and saints of God are given to know the mysteries, because these individuals give up everything to follow Jesus and do God's will. The mysteries are the hidden things and/or religious secrets confided only to the initiated and not to ordinary mortals. The initiated are those who were predestined to adoption as sons and daughters by Jesus Christ to God. "For whom He [God] foreknew, He also predestined to be conformed to the image of His Son, that He might be the firstborn among many brethren. Moreover whom He predestined, these He also called; whom He called, these He also justified; and whom He justified, and these He also glorified" Romans 8:29-30 (NKJV). It is also important to know that many were called by God, but only a few were chosen. "For many are called, but few are chosen" Matthew 22:14 (NKJV).

The mysteries of God's Kingdom are the parables Jesus taught and prophesied to His followers. One of His mysteries revealed that some believers, those who have been born-again and sealed with the Holy Spirit, will _quench_ God's Spirit and _will not_ be allowed into the wedding feast. This is clearly illustrated in the parable of the wedding feast. Subsequently, these individuals _will not_ inherit _eternal life_ as promised by God! As revealed in Scripture, "Do not quench the Spirit" 1 Thessalonians 5:19 (NKJV). This is a spiritual dynamic not taught by many of God's servants because many of them do not hear, see nor understand the things God's Spirit is saying to the church. They understand that the Holy Spirit can be quenched, but few teach about the behaviors of the flesh that causes this shortfall! Seeking the things of this world means to be engaged in the things offered by the god of this world, Satan. Make no mistake...; all creation is of this world. Jesus reminded us that we are of this world, but He is not. "And He said to them, "You are from beneath; I am from above. You are of this world; I am not of this world" John 8:23 (NKJV). Neither is Jesus' Kingdom, the Kingdom of God of this world. "Jesus answered, "My kingdom is not of this world. If My kingdom were of this world, My servants would fight, so that I should not be delivered to the Jews; but now My kingdom is not from here" John 18:36 (NKJV).

For this world only offers only a craving for physical pleasure, a craving for the things we see, and pride in our achievements and obtaining possessions. Those who love the Lord have faith in Him and are obedient to God's Word. They have been transformed from this world with its lust, pride, and vanity because these individuals and have learned to crucify these behaviors! "And those who are Christ's have crucified the flesh with its passions and desires" Galatians 5:24 (NKJV). The putting off of the flesh with its passions and lusts is the condition of those sold out to Christ Jesus. It is the mortifying or subduing of the flesh by these believers as they walk in total faith. These individuals are being transformed from this world through the renewing of their minds. "And do not be conformed to this world, but be transformed by the renewing of your mind, that you may prove what is that good and acceptable and perfect will of God" Romans 12:2 (NKJV). Now they are *citizens* of God's Kingdom through Jesus Christ, who is the King!

Please understand that lust and pride are of this world. These ungodly attributes drive believers to forsake what they have learned about the Father, Jesus the Son and the Holy Spirit. These individuals allow Satan and his angels to influence and deceive them to partake of riotous living that benefits the flesh and not the soul! Furthermore, the works of the flesh *quench* the Spirit of God. "Now the works of the flesh are evident, which are: adultery, fornication, uncleanness, lewdness, idolatry, sorcery, hatred, contentions, jealousies, outbursts of wrath, selfish ambitions, dissensions, heresies, envy, murders, drunkenness, revelries, and the like; of which I tell you beforehand, just as I also told you in time past, that those who practice such things will not inherit the kingdom of God" Galatians 5:19-21 (NKJV).

Metaphorically, *quenching* the Holy Spirit means to *extinguish*, to *suppress* and to *stifle* the believer of divine influence. It is like putting something on a fire to put it out! John the Baptist told his followers, "I indeed baptize you with water unto repentance, but He [Jesus] who is coming after me is mightier than I, whose sandals I am not worthy to carry. He will baptize you with the Holy Spirit and fire" Matthew 3:11 (NKJV). The Holy Spirit is the third person of the triune God. The Holy Spirit is co-equal and co-eternal with the Father and the Son. He influences the believer and gives him or her power to feel, think and make decisions according to God's Will. Scripture makes it clear that everyone receives the Holy Spirit the moment he or she believes in Jesus Christ. "In Him you also trusted, after you heard the word of truth, the gospel of your salvation; in whom also, having believed, you were sealed with the Holy Spirit of promise, who is the guarantee of our inheritance until the redemption of the purchased possession, to the praise of His glory" Ephesians 1:13-14 (NKJV). Believers may be sealed by the Holy Spirit until the day of redemption, but they can still _quench_ the Spirit by their unrighteous living which suppresses (to curtail or stop the activities thereof) God's Divine power in their lives.

The primary purpose of God's Spirit in human flesh is to transform the believer's life into the image and likeness of Jesus Christ. It is the task of the Holy Spirit to comfort, lead, direct and impart truth to the believer in accordance with God's calling and purpose. God's Spirit also produces spiritual fruit in the believer's life which advances God's Kingdom. "But the fruit of the Spirit is love, joy, peace, longsuffering, kindness, goodness, faithfulness, gentleness, self-control. Against such there is no law. And those who are Christ's have crucified the flesh with its passions and desires" Galatians 5:22-24 (NKJV). As long as a believer remains Spirit-filled, obeys God' Word, bears spiritual fruit and do not quench the Holy Spirit, he or she will be ready to meet the Lord on that great day! However, those who _quench_ God's Spirit lusting after and engaging in the things of the world will not be allowed into the wedding feast. The door will be shut as revealed in the parable of the ten virgins (Matthew chapter 25).

The mystery (parable) of the ten virgins is extremely important to the body of Christ because it reveals the nature of Christ's return, those born-again believers who _will be ready_ to meet Him and the essence of their preparation. Jesus' prophecy of the ten virgins reveals major facts regarding the last days which the body of Christ has already begun to experience! Jesus prophesied that many Christians would quench the Divine power of the Holy Spirit in their lives; that the body of Christ (the church) would slumber and sleep (be negligent, careless, yield to sloth and sin); and that the wedding feast would be closed to those who succumb to the lust and desires of their flesh.

We already see a multitude of false ministers and teachers in the body of Christ who teach fables instead of the full council of God's Word! These grievous individuals seek wealth, power and popularity. The Apostle Peter, along with others, warned us of these ravenous wolves (in the clothing of false shepherds) who come in sheep's clothing. "But there were also false prophets in Israel, just as there will be false teachers among you. They will cleverly teach destructive heresies and even deny the Master who bought them. In this way, they will bring sudden destruction on themselves. Many will follow their evil teaching and shameful immorality. And because of these teachers, the way of truth will be slandered. In their greed they will make up clever lies to get hold of your money. But God condemned them long ago, and their destruction will not be delayed" 2 Peter 2:1-3 (NLT).

I know the church world keep hearing how *good things are going to be* from these false prophets. You have been hearing that message for years, but it is not supported by the words of Jesus. He prophesied to His disciples and the rest of His body that we would be arrested, persecuted, and killed. We would be hated all over the world because we are Jesus' followers and He said, "These things must come to pass! "And Jesus answered and said to them: "Take heed that no one deceives you. For many will come in My name, saying, 'I am the Christ,' and will deceive many. And you will hear of wars and rumors of wars. See that you are not troubled; for all these things must come to pass, but the end is not yet. For nation will rise against nation, and kingdom against kingdom. And there will be famines, pestilences, and earthquakes in various places. All these are the beginning of sorrows. "Then they will deliver you up to tribulation and kill you, and you will be hated by all nations for My name's sake. And then many will be offended, will betray one another, and will hate one another. Then many false prophets will rise up and deceive many. And because lawlessness will abound, the love of many will grow cold. But he who endures to the end shall be saved." Matthew 24:4-13 (NKJV).

We already know that things are getting worse. We see how this world is deteriorating and how perverse people are becoming! However, we should not despair because we knew from the curse what thorns and thistles would bring forth for us. Thorns and thistles represent the trials, tests, afflictions, sorrows, the Lord's chastisements, hardships and suffering in our lives. Now the end of the age will conclude with the Tribulation Period. Does this sound like everything is going to get better? God's people have always been in a state to judge and examine themselves because a *tree is judged by its fruit*. "Either make the tree good and its fruit good, or else make the tree bad and its fruit bad; for a tree is known by its fruit" Matthew 12:33 (NKJV). He and she, who have ears to hear, hear what the Spirit is saying to the church!

As you can see, the church has certainly been asleep! Consequently, there has been little or no *witness* from the unified church (the Body of Christ) against the ever-changing landscape of the world's morality. The LGBT (lesbian, gay, bi-sexual, transgender) community has a greater voice in the land than millions of silent Christians! Whenever a faithful believer stands against this type immorality and speaks the truth of God's Word, he or she is ostracized. Same sex marriages have become law with only a minor challenge from God's people. What would have happened if Christians would have responded in masses throughout the United States against the proposal of such a law? Surely the Supreme Court and our national representatives would have been pressured to not support such an abomination in relationship to God's Word. Perhaps just this kind of effort would have caused some to seek God in this matter.

Now I realize that just taking a stance against this form of fornication (adultery, homosexuality, lesbianism, intercourse with animals etc.) is not going to stop it, for this indulgence has been on the earth as long as the earth has existed. Nevertheless, the Word of God would be raised as the standard for God's judgement. Furthermore, we have our children and the next generation to think of. God said in Genesis: "Be fruitful and fill the earth." Do not be deceived, a same sex union cannot produce the next generation. He further said, "Train up a child in the way he should go, and when he is old he will not depart from it" Proverbs 22:6 (NKJV). People will do as they please and will be judged accordingly. Please keep this in mind, before the world was formed God foreknew those He predestined and called as His elect people. God's elect are all of the believers of Jesus Christ. Even though *many were called*, only *a few will be chosen* because of whom these believers would ultimately *choose to obey!* "Don't you realize that you become the slave of whatever you choose to obey? You can be a slave to sin, which leads to death, or you can choose to obey God, which leads to righteous living" Romans 6:16 (NLT). It is not how you start the race for *life* in God's Kingdom, but it's how you finish!

THE PARABLE (*MYSTERY*) OF THE WISE AND FOOLISH VIRGINS!

Jesus spoke unto His followers many mysteries (parables) of the Kingdom of God. Each parable is important to know and to discern spiritually because they reveal secrets relative to how the body of Christ should live while on this earth! None are more important than the parable of the ten virgins! This parable reveals the evolution of the good seeds, the sons of the Kingdom, as well as, the tares, the sons of the wicked one, as depicted in the parable of the wheat and the tares. "The field is the world, the good seeds are the sons of the kingdom, but the tares are the sons of the wicked one" Matthew 13:38 (NKJV). See the parable of the ten virgins below:

> *"Then the kingdom of heaven shall be likened to ten virgins who took their lamps and went out to meet the bridegroom. Now five of them were wise, and five were foolish. Those who were foolish took their lamps and took no oil with them, but the wise took oil in their vessels with their lamps. But while the bridegroom was delayed, they all slumbered and slept.*
>
> *"And at midnight a cry was heard: 'Behold, the bridegroom is coming; go out to meet him!' Then all those virgins arose and trimmed their lamps. And the foolish said to the wise, 'Give us some of your oil, for our lamps are going out.' But the wise answered, saying, 'No, lest there should not be enough for us and you; but go rather to those who sell, and buy for yourselves.' And while*

they went to buy, the bridegroom came, and those who were ready went in with him to the wedding; and the door was shut.

"Afterward the other virgins came also, saying, 'Lord, Lord, open to us!' But he answered and said, 'Assuredly, I say to you, I do not know you.' "Watch therefore, for you know neither the day nor the hour in which the Son of Man is coming" Matthew 25:1-13 (NKJV).

The Parable of The Ten Virgins Explained!
God's Kingdom in heaven and on earth shall be like ten virgins. The ten virgins are figuratively of the local church in its relation to Christ. A virgin is metaphorically of a chaste person as revealed in Revelation 14:4 (NKJV) – "These are the ones who were not defiled with women, for they are virgins. These are the ones who follow the Lamb wherever He goes. These were redeemed from among men, being first fruits to God and to the Lamb." However, the Apostle Paul was concerned that some of their minds were corrupted and were _conforming_ to this world. He said, "For I am jealous for you with godly jealousy. For I have betrothed you to one husband, that I may present you as a chaste virgin to Christ. But I fear, lest somehow, as the serpent deceived Eve by his craftiness, so your minds may be corrupted from the simplicity that is in Christ" 2 Corinthians 11:2-3 (NKJV).

The corruption spoken of by the Apostle Paul is to destroy by means of corrupting and bringing into a worse state. Corruption, in this instance, means the significance of destroying and marring a local church by leading it away from that condition of knowledge, holiness of life and purity of doctrine. In an ethical sense, it is to corrupt or deprave. When I first read about the simplicity that is in Christ, I wondered if there was really such a thing. Yes, there is such a thing and it is salvation comes to those who _love_ Jesus, have total _faith_ in Him and are _obedient_ to God's Word. We have made the Gospel complex by teaching everything else, but judgement will qualify these three things in a person's life. We can talk about whatever, but if you do not 1) love the Lord, 2) have genuine faith in Him and 3) are obedient to the Word of God, then enjoy this world as best you can because relative life ends here!

Paul was concerned that the church of God at Corinth would be deceived like Eve was deceived. Jesus was equally concerned and warned God's people of the magnitude of deception amongst God's people through false prophets and teachers that would permeate the world in the last days. He said, "Then many false prophets will rise up and deceive many" Matthew 24:11 (NKJV). The Apostle Peter also revealed the destructive doctrine that would be rampant in the last days! Peter stated, "But there were also false prophets among the people, even as there will be false teachers among you, who will secretly bring in destructive heresies, even denying the Lord who bought them, and bring on themselves swift destruction" 2 Peter 2:1 (NKJV). The definition of deception is to cause one to believe what is not true; to mislead and render that which gives a false impression, whether by appearance, statement or influence. Deception is accomplished through empty words, false impressions and belittling the true character of sin.

The Bible tells us that false teachers and ministers will grow in number and deceive many, yet many Christians will continue to drink from the well of their *devious doctrines*. "But evil people and impostors will flourish. They will deceive others and will themselves be deceived "But evil men and impostors will grow worse and worse, deceiving and being deceived" 2 Timothy 3:13 (NKJV). In the moral or ethical sense, these individual are evil and wicked servants of God. Here are the dangers of the last days. "You should know this Timothy that in the last days there will be very difficult times. For people will love only themselves and their money. They will be boastful and proud, scoffing at God, disobedient to their parents, and ungrateful. They will consider nothing sacred. They will be unloving and unforgiving; they will slander others and have no self-control. They will be cruel and hate what is good. They will betray their friends, be reckless, be puffed up with pride, and love pleasure rather than God. They will act religious, but they will reject the power that could make them godly. *Stay away from people like that*" 2 Timothy 3:1-5 (NLT)! If you do not understand this truth, you will never understand the revelation of the ten virgins.

The wise virgins, today's saints of God, took their lamps and went out to meet the bridegroom (Jesus Christ). Their lamps are symbolic of a torch which shines: A light within them that reveals the image and likeness of Christ. "You are the light of the world. A city that is set on a hill cannot be hidden" Matthew 5:14 (NKJV). The lamb also reveals the spiritual readiness of the believer. Because lambs are small, they frequently need replenishing and the oil is a symbol of the Holy Spirit. Perhaps, now you can understand why Christians need constant re-filling with God's Spirit to be perpetually Spirit-filled. Many times believers live without the anointing power of the Holy Spirit, because they have either grieved or quenched God's Spirit by their life styles. The Bible speaks of the many ways Christians allow themselves to be deceived by Satan. It occurs when believers _seek_ the things of this world and/or allow their sinful nature to dominate their lifestyles and behaviors through the desire and lust of the flesh.

Deception and lust are the reasons there is a constant battle between the flesh and the Holy Spirit. "For the flesh lusts against the Spirit, and the Spirit against the flesh; and these are contrary to one another, so that you do not do the things that you wish" Galatians 5:17 (NKJV). The term, filling of the Spirit is really a command to obey! The filling of the Holy Spirit is not our having more of the Holy Spirit, but the Holy Spirit having more of us! In other words, it is when the Holy Spirit controls and/or commands our mind, body, soul and spirit. The Spirit guides and teaches you in the things of God. The more Spirit-controlled you are, the more you respond to the ways of God. You will also bear spiritual fruit and demonstrate greater Christ-likeness in your behaviors and deeds. Believers choose to be filled with God's Spirit by surrendering their wills to Jesus and putting on the full armor of God.

Filling of the Holy Spirit is not like the indwelling of the Holy Spirit. Indwelling is what happens when a person first believes in Jesus Christ. They are sealed by the Spirit until the Day of Redemption. "And do not grieve the Holy Spirit of God, by whom you were sealed for the day of redemption" Ephesians 4:30 (NKJV). Filling occurs more and more as the individual surrenders to the guidance of the Spirit and/or after a believer has grieved and/or quenched God's Spirit, but repents in their heart and asked the Lord for forgiveness. Once an individual repents, they are expected to turn from their wicked ways and live an obedient life before the Lord!

As the believer continues to grow in obedience to God's Word, to His calling, laws, covenants, and His will, the more God's Spirit is able to comfort, lead, guide and teach the believer all things. This *is* the filling of the Holy Spirit! Additionally, filling of the Spirit is the bestowing of comfort, joy and peace; it is also spiritual knowledge, revelation, fruits of righteousness and the knowledge of God's will. Furthermore, the Spirit shall bestow all your needs with abundance through material supplies. "And my God shall supply all your need according to His riches in glory by Christ Jesus" Philippians 4:19 (NKJV).

Now five of the virgins were wise, and five were foolish. Those who were foolish took their lamps and took no oil with them, but the wise virgins took oil in their vessels *with* their lamps. This Scripture is important to understanding why some virgins were considered *wise* and some *foolish!* The wise virgins lived according to the Holy Spirit. The foolish virgins were without God's Spirit and therefore lived according to their carnal mind and flesh. Now the lambs of the wise virgins were symbolic of their light which is their witness and the demonstration of their citizenship in the Kingdom of God. Wise virgins demonstrate the image and character of Jesus as they let their light shine. As stated above, "You are the light of the world when the Holy Spirit lives in you to lead and guide your steps. The oil in their lambs is representative of the Holy Spirit. It is the *Spirit that gives power* from on high and enables the believer to be a shining light in the spiritual darkness of this world.

Jesus made known that the wise virgins (saints of God) took oil in their vessels *with* their lamps which meant they lived according to the guidance of God's Spirit and God's anointing. *Please do not miss this!* The wise virgins (saints) took *oil in the vessels* with their light. They were vessels! Vessels denote a small receptacle, pail or reservoir for carrying oil. The small vessel/reservoir represents a faithful believer who lives as directed by God's Spirit. As mentioned earlier, because the vessels are small, refilling is necessary from time to time. This is indicative of the fact that we all sin and fall short of God's glory. Therefore, it is necessary to recognize the sin, ask the Lord for forgiveness with a contrite heart, turn from the sin, continue to pray and ask the Lord for the filling of God's Spirit. Also remember that Spirit-filled believers are free from indwelling sin as shown in the next Scripture. "There is therefore now no condemnation to those who are in Christ Jesus, who do not walk according to the flesh, but according to the Spirit" Romans 8:1 (NKJV). Hence, the wise saints were born-again Christians and baptized by God's Spirit and they lived according to the Spirit everywhere they went. Therefore, they were able to produce a good light and a good witness which is symbolic of the lamp.

The foolish virgins took their lamps (their light and witness) and took no oil (the Holy Spirit) with them. Please understand this: The foolish virgins were also born-again Christians and baptized by God's Spirit at some earlier point-in-time. However, during their course of life, they apparently *grieved* and *quenched* the Holy Spirit. In their apparent sin, they did not repent, ask for forgiveness and turn from their wicked ways; this not only grieves God's Spirit, but quenches the Spirit when the believer continues *to practice* the sin! At judgment time, Jesus will say to those Christians who have quenched God's Spirit, "And then I will declare to them, 'I never knew you; depart from Me, you who practice lawlessness" Matthew 7:23 (NKJV)!

This is the reason the Holy Spirit becomes inactive in a believer's life. "And do not grieve the Holy Spirit of God, by whom you were sealed for the day of redemption" Ephesians 4:30 (NKJV). "Do not quench the Spirit" 1 Thessalonians 5:19 (NKJV). Metaphorically, quenching the Spirit is to suppress and stifle the believer of divine influence. As mentioned before, quenching is like putting something (i.e., water) on a fire to extinguish it and to hinder its operations. Quenching the Spirit means the believer is without God's guidance, comfort, anointing, and wisdom; plus he or she is then separated from God like man was after his disobedience in the garden.

Separation from God by not living according to His Spirit is a *major deficiency* in God's economy. God Spirit indwells those who believe in His Son and trust Him for spiritual guidance, truth and power. Whenever a believer quenches His Spirit, they separate themselves from God and are no longer operating by the Spirit, but by their flesh! Those who are still under the control of their sinful nature (the flesh) can never please God! If God's Spirit ceases to function in a believer, for whatever reason, that individual no longer belongs to Jesus. "But you are not controlled by your sinful nature. You are controlled by the Spirit *if* you have the Spirit of God living in you. (And remember that those who do not have the Spirit of Christ living in them do not belong to him at all.)" - Romans 8:9 (NLT). Furthermore, because believers become the *temple of God* when the Spirit lives in them, God will destroy anyone who *defiles* that temple. "Do you not know that you are the temple of God and that the Spirit of God dwells in you? If anyone defiles the temple of God, God will destroy him. For the temple of God is holy, which temple you are" 1 Corinthians 3:16- (NKJV). There are a multitude of Christians who are unaware of this truth who defile God's Spirit without knowing what they have done!

At any rate, the bridegroom (Jesus Christ) delayed His coming and they all *slumbered* and *slept*. It is interesting to know that *they all* slumbered and slept. This is indicative of the church in the last days; it means all Christians, both good and bad, went to sleep. It is when the voice and/or demonstration of the church become silent and there is little or no witness of the character of Christ in the earth. The church continues to operate as a body of believers, but they do little to challenge the moral conscience of this perverse world. Slumbered means they became negligent and careless. Metaphorically, the word *slumbered* means the destruction awaiting false teachers. *Sleep*, on the other hand, metaphorically means to yield to sloth and sin and to be indifferent to one's salvation. Long story short, as Jesus delays His second coming, the church (the body of Christ) becomes no different than those in the world. They yield to sloth and sin, which is the quality or state of being lazy and they transgress. We understand that *sin* is to miss or wander from the path of uprightness and honor. It is to do or go wrong! Here are three other definitions for sin: 1) To wander from the law of God; 2) To violate God's law and 3) To commit sin which is also the transgression of the law of God (disobedience).

At midnight, a cry is heard for behold the bridegroom is coming; let us go out to meet him! The Lord Himself will come down from heaven with a commanding shout! "For the Lord Himself will descend from heaven with a shout, with the voice of an archangel, and with the trumpet of God. And the dead in Christ will rise first" 1 Thessalonians 4:16 (NKJV). The cry is a shout of command denoting the Lord will descend from heaven for the saints (those who have fallen asleep and the living) to meet for Him in the air (the rapture of the church). Then all those virgins arose and trimmed their lamps. The word *trim* is symbolic of putting things in order, to arrange, make ready and be prepared for the Lord's coming! Trimming their lamps is making sure they are doing the work of the Kingdom and being good stewards of God's calling in their lives.

Now the foolish said to the wise, "Give us some of your oil, for our lamps are going out. But the wise answered, saying, 'No, lest there should not be enough for us and you; but go rather to those who sell, and buy for yourselves.' Here lies significant spiritual insight and truth of which few believers are aware! The wise virgins tell the foolish virgins, they are in no position to share the Holy Spirit with them. Furthermore, they should go to the market place to those who buy and sell! The wise virgins directed the foolish virgins to go back to the places where they had lived, operated and traded. Trading is the activity of buying and selling goods or services. It is one of the major activities of the world. Trade is one of the greatest gifts that Lucifer introduced, established and organized in the earth that corrupts the minds and hearts of those who indulge in it. Hear God's words to Lucifer: "With your wisdom and your understanding you have gained riches for yourself, and gathered gold and silver into your treasuries; by your great wisdom in trade you have increased your riches, and your heart is lifted up because of your riches" Ezekiel 28:4-5 (NKJV).

Never forget that Satan is the god of this world and he influences the world, even God's people to share in his riches. The tares, sons of the wicked one, Satan's ministers of righteousness that have infiltrated the church and caused great sins of greed, pride, selfishness, and a spirit of control. These behaviors deride from acquisitiveness (having a strong desire to own or acquire more things), covetousness (having a craving for possession), gluttony (greedy or excessive indulgence), materialism (a way of thinking that gives too much importance to material possessions rather than to spiritual or intellectual things) and more! The market place represents the world of greed, pride, selfishness, and lust. Unfortunately, the church has entered this area of greed through the buying and selling of spiritual materials and activities. Marketing of these items does help the church's finances when they are done properly and in order! However, massive marketing in the house of prayer is the very thing that upset Jesus Christ before. "Then Jesus went into the temple of God and drove out all those who bought and sold in the temple, and overturned the tables of the money changers and the seats of those who sold doves. And He said to them, "It is written, 'My house shall be called a house of prayer,' but you have made it a 'den of thieves" Matthew 21:12-13 (NKJV). We missed the message Jesus was conveying because the church is doing it again; we are marketing and selling material goods in the house of God for profit! Unfortunately, today's sale of goods is creating an abundance of greed, pride and selfishness in many churches.

Many of God's servants have yet to realize the wickedness and dangers of engaging in the addictions of this world. Trade does the same thing to Christians as it did to Lucifer and those who do it for a living. It stimulates lust, greed, pride and other ungodly behaviors that violate God's Word! I believe many of today's servants have become millionaires from the trades of the church instead of having proper acquisitions of goods that benefits those in need such as the homeless, the poor, those caught-up in trafficking and other human deficiencies. Grievous trade is truly the way of the world and not the Kingdom of God. Individuals who develop this type character and behavior are duplicating the lusts and character of the god of this world. Lucifer was a master at greed, trade and wealth. Just because things are done in the name of the Lord does not make them right. Especially when the practice becomes an activity that produces greed, trade and wealth, pride, selfishness, and a lust to get more and more! Jesus said, "My Temple will be called a house of prayer,' but you have turned it into a den of thieves" Matthew 21:13 (NLT)! The house of God is holy and we must keep it holy!

The foolish virgins had their lamps (a light), but their witness (their light) represented lust, greed, selfishness, pride, trade and wealth. Their witness was a clear demonstration of the character of the sons of the tares. Unfortunately, many of God's people seek the Lord and His Kingdom early in their Christians lives; however because of greed, as God blesses them, they become sons of the wicked-one as revealed in the parable of the wheat and tares. They begin to lust after wealth and popularity! The sad part of this scenario is the number of God's people who refuse to perceive and discern this spiritual metamorphosis that is occurring in the church and has been occurring for hundreds of years. A multitude of Christian leaders and congregants have evolved into false preachers, teachers and workers. These individuals seek the things of this world instead of the things of God's Kingdom. "For such are false apostles, deceitful workers, transforming themselves into apostles of Christ. And no wonder! For Satan himself transforms himself into an angel of light. Therefore it is no great thing if his ministers also transform themselves into ministers of righteousness, whose end will be according to their works" 2 Corinthians 11:13-15 (NKJV). Because these virgins were no longer Spirit-filled, they light represented something other than the image of Jesus Christ and His Kingdom.

And while the foolish virgins chased after their wealth and riches, the bridegroom (Jesus Christ) came, and those who _were ready_ went in with Him to the wedding feast and the door was shut! The wise virgins, who live by faith and the power of God's Spirit, were ready for their witness of the Kingdom of God and His righteousness. They had become living sacrifices, holy and acceptable to the Lord. These individuals were those whose lives had been transformed by the power of God.

"All praise to God, the Father of our Lord Jesus Christ. It is by his great mercy that we have been born again, because God raised Jesus Christ from the dead. Now we live with great expectation, and we have a priceless inheritance—an inheritance that is kept in heaven for you, pure and undefiled, beyond the reach of change and decay. And through your faith, God is protecting you by his power until you receive this salvation, which is ready to be revealed on the last day for all to see.

So be truly glad. There is wonderful joy ahead, even though you must endure many trials for a little while. These trials will show that your faith is genuine. It is being tested as fire tests and purifies gold—though your faith is far more precious than mere gold. So when your faith remains strong through many trials, it will bring you much praise and glory and honor on the day when Jesus Christ is revealed to the whole world" 1 Peter 1:3-7 (NLT).

These believers were the ones identified as *bad and good* in the parable of the marriage feast. The bad were those maligned by Satan. They were those who had illnesses and evil spirits, but the Lord had healed them and restored sight to those who were the blind. The good were those of a good constitution or nature, upright, honorable who were pleasant, agreeable, joyful and happy. Those who *were ready* went in with Him to the wedding feast and the door was shut! The door is of reference to the door of the kingdom of heaven (likened to a palace) that denotes the conditions which must be complied with in order to be received into the kingdom of God. Shutting this door is metaphorically obstructing the entrance into the kingdom of heaven.

When the other *Christians* came and attempted to get in the wedding feast, Jesus answered and said, 'Assuredly, I say to you, I do not know you. He didn't know them because their light was unrighteous and they had not prepared themselves for His return. Jesus prophesied this event in other Scriptures and the same results occurred! He prophesied how the true way into the Kingdom would be for several of His servants who were called into the five-fold ministry. "And He Himself gave some to be apostles, some prophets, some evangelists, and some pastors and teachers" Ephesians 4:11 (NKJV). Jesus also told them, "I never knew you. Get away from me, you who break God's laws." He said, "Not everyone who says to Me, 'Lord, Lord,' shall enter the kingdom of heaven, but he who does the will of My Father in heaven. Many will say to Me in that day, 'Lord, Lord, have we not prophesied in Your name, cast out demons in Your name, and done many wonders in Your name?' And then I will declare to them, 'I never knew you; depart from Me, you who practice lawlessness" Matthew 7:21-23 (NKJV).

There was also the time when Jesus prophesied His response to Christian followers. Again, they were met with the same response. This time Jesus responded, "When once the Master of the house has risen up and shut the door, and you begin to stand outside and knock at the door, saying, 'Lord, Lord, open for us,' and He will answer and say to you, 'I do not know you, where are you from,' then you will begin to say, 'We ate and drank in Your presence, and You taught in our streets.' But He will say, 'I tell you I do not know you, where are you from. Depart from Me, all you workers of iniquity" Luke 13:25-27 (NKJV). That day will represent a sad time in the economy of man's time on the earth. However, it will be too late to do anything about it! Jesus advises His people to watch and pray now *while we have the chance!* He says to us, "Watch therefore, for you know neither the day nor the hour in which the Son of Man is coming" Matthew 25:1-13 (NKJV).

Maybe it is just me... but it seems that only a few Christians are really concerned about the final judgment day and whether they are truly saved. Personally, I do not see many Christians pressing through the circumstances of life to achieve citizenship in God's Kingdom. There are many obstacles on the earth that can discourage a believer from fulfilling his/her calling in life. As revealed earlier, all these things are part of God's Divine order to test the hearts of humankind as result of the disobedience in the Garden of Eden. These tribulations, thorns and thistles, hardships and sufferings all tests our faith, love and obedience in Jesus Christ and in God's Word! Therefore, God's Kingdom does suffer violence! God's true and faithful people must press through and endure these circumstances of life to enter and/or inherit the Kingdom! There are many obstacles in the pathway to God's Kingdom. Listed below are many of these obstacles that God's people must endure and overcome in their daily lives. These obstacles can deceive, discourage and cause even God's elect to give up!

THE KINGDOM OF GOD SUFFERS VIOLENCE!
Unknown to many Christian believers is the fact that the curse caused God's people to become the living sacrifices, holy and acceptable to Him! The afflictions and sufferings of earth do not occur by accident; they are part of God's Divine will for humans. A living sacrifice is a *victim!* A

victim is one who is harmed by or made to suffer under a circumstance or condition. Sacrificing is the act of giving up something highly valued for the sake of something else considered to be of greater value or claim. We become victims as we live through the fiery trials that are set forth to test us. "Beloved, do not think it strange concerning the fiery trial which is to try you, as though some strange thing happened to you; but rejoice to the extent that you partake of Christ's sufferings, that when His glory is revealed, you may also be glad with exceeding joy" 1 Peter 4:12-13 (NKJV). The Apostle James stated, "My brethren, count it all joy when you fall into various trials, knowing that the testing of your faith produces patience. But let patience have its perfect work, that you may be perfect and complete, lacking nothing. If any of you lacks wisdom, let him ask of God, who gives to all liberally and without reproach, and it will be given to him" James 1:2-5 (NKJV).

These trials occur for *our sake* which is the statement God gave to Adam. "Then to Adam He said, "Because you have heeded the voice of your wife, and have eaten from the tree of which I commanded you, saying, 'You shall not eat of it': "Cursed is the ground *for your sake*; in toil [pain, labor, hardship, sorrow, strife] you shall eat of it all the days of your life" Genesis 3:17 (NKJV). As faithful believers endure these adversities of life, we are developed and matured in the ways of God as sons and daughters. Enduring these adversities through the help of Jesus Christ and the power of God's Spirit faithful believers are able to crucify their flesh. "And those who are Christ's have crucified the flesh with its passions and desires" Galatians 5:24 (NKJV). Furthermore, Jesus said, "But he who endures to the end shall be saved" Matthew 24:13 (NKJV). So, the Kingdom of God does suffer violence and the violent believer takes the Kingdom by force through pressing!

Obstacles to Inheriting God's Kingdom!

From previous discussions, we already know God's *curse* serves as an obstacle because God's people must work through the adversities of thorns and thistles set forth by Him for the earth.

- Even though God's curse set forth obstacles that humankind would have to endure and overcome, the Apostle Paul put everything in perspective. He recorded, "For I consider that the sufferings of this present time are not worthy to be compared with the glory which shall be revealed in us" Romans 8:18 (NKJV). We know that all creation was made subject to *vanity*, yet through the power of Jesus Christ and God's Spirit, humankind can be delivered from the bondage of corruption, so there is a way to become worthy children for God. "For the creature was made subject to vanity, not willingly, but by reason of him who hath subjected the same in hope, because the creature itself also shall be delivered from the bondage of corruption into the glorious liberty of the children of God" Romans 8:20-21 (KJV).

- Because of vanity, selfishness, greed, control, pride, and other wicked behaviors, one of the greatest obstacles to inheriting God's Kingdom is our *flesh!* The flesh of humans is wicked for the thoughts of our hearts are continually evil! "Then the Lord saw that the wickedness of man was great in the earth, and that every intent of the thoughts of his heart was only evil continually. And the Lord was sorry that He had made man on the earth, and He was grieved in His heart" Genesis 6:5-6 (NKJV). Humankind, even Christians seldom examine themselves to know who they really are. Therefore, the wickedness of their flesh is overlooked which means, out-of-sight, out-of-mind! This is the reason there is a battle between God's Spirit and human flesh. "I say then: Walk in the Spirit, and you shall not fulfill the lust of the flesh. For the flesh lusts against the Spirit and the Spirit against the flesh; and these are contrary to one another, so that you do not do the things that you wish. But if you are led by the Spirit, you are not under the law" Galatians 5:16-18 (NKJV).

- The works of our flesh are obstacles to entering the Kingdom of God. Those who practice such things, the works of the flesh, will not inherit the Kingdom! "Now the works of the flesh are evident, which are: adultery, fornication, uncleanness, lewdness, idolatry, sorcery, hatred, contentions, jealousies, outbursts of wrath, self-ish ambitions, dissensions, heresies, envy, murders, drunkenness, revelries, and the like; of which I tell you beforehand, just as I also told you in time past, that those who practice such things will not inherit the kingdom of God" Galatians 5:19-21 (NKJV).

• Satan and his angels are the foremost obstacles to the Kingdom of God. They deceive humankind far more than Christians realize! I wish the body of Christ would discern the true level of human deception; only a few believers have given it much thought. It would be different if God's servants would preach and teach the truth of human deception and the wickedness of the human heart. However, because Satan's minsters have infiltrated the church, they are persistent in preaching and teaching false doctrine. These individuals have become Satan's ministers of righteousness. "For such are false apostles, deceitful workers, transforming them-selves into apostles of Christ. And no wonder! For Satan himself transforms himself into an angel of light. Therefore it is no great thing if his ministers also transform themselves into ministers of righteousness, whose end will be according to their works" 2 Corinthians 11:13-15 (NKJV). They look like, talk like and preach like men and women of God, but they are wolves in sheep's cloth-ing. "Beware of false prophets who come disguised as harmless sheep but are really vicious wolves" Matthew 7:15 (NLT). These individuals defile God's temples (the saints of God) and will be destroyed by Him. "God will destroy anyone who destroys this temple. For God's temple is holy, and you are that temple" 1 Corinthians 3:17 (NLT). The temples of God are the saints of God who have given themselves to loving, trusting and obeying Jesus Christ.

• Faithful believers _must_ suffer many tribulations to enter God's Kingdom. "Strengthening the souls of the disciples, exhorting them to continue in the faith, and saying, "We must through many tribulations enter the kingdom of God" Acts 14:22 (NKJV). These tribulations are appointed and destined by God in the fullness of

His time! These hardships come to establish believers and encourage them concerning their faith. "Therefore, when we could no longer endure it, we thought it good to be left in Athens alone, and sent Timothy, our brother and minister of God, and our fellow laborer in the gospel of Christ, to establish you and encourage you concerning your faith, that no one should be shaken by these afflictions; for you yourselves know that we are appointed to this. For, in fact, we told you before when we were with you that we would suffer tribulation, just as it happened, and you know" Thessalonians 3:1-4 (NKJV).

Tribulations, afflictions, sorrows, hardships and sufferings also test your faith! To some, these tribulations become a stumbling block. "But he who received the seed on stony places, this is he who hears the word and immediately receives it with joy; yet he has no root in himself, but endures only for a while. For when tribulation or persecution arises because of the word, immediately he stumbles" Matthew 13:20-21 (NKJV). The appointment of afflictions is divinely ordained by God to develop and mature faithful believers in the ways of God. These tribulations mature them in their love, faith and obedience to Jesus Christ.

The proliferation of false Christian leaders is a *major obstacle* for the body of Christ (church) in our quest to obtain truth. Regrettably, the church seems to have no clue of the multitude of false teachers and preachers that have defiled the household of faith. The proliferation (rapid growth and production) is truly overwhelming. Believers need to take-to-heart the prophesies spoken by Jesus, Paul, Peter, John and Jude. They warned of the influx of false leaders to come to the church. They desperately attempted to warn the church of the last day period when many false leaders would infiltrate the church and cause havoc. It is now up to faithful believers to discern those who deliver false doctrine and slander the Word of God with clever lies, to get hold of their money. They gave heed to Jewish fables and the commandments of men like the scribes and Pharisees did! Jewish fables are narratives that were set forth and are in fact falsifications. The commandments of men is that which is imposed by decree or law; a precept. Many of today's ministers skew the truth of the Bible to fit their needs and theology.

Why would so many of God's servants record prophesies in His Word (The Bible) about the advent of false prophets, teachers and ministers if it were not going to be a major problem in these last days? Many Christians live under these conditions and are either blind to the situation or just overlook it due to their relationship with the church leader. Whatever the reason, now is the time to heed God's Word because these individuals are affecting the salvation of many congregants, perhaps *even you!* Shown below are biblical Scriptures regarding false teaching.

- This is part of Jesus' message to His disciples regarding the last day events - *"Then many false prophets will rise up and deceive many" - Matthew 24:11 (NKJV).*
- Here is a Scripture recorded in 1 John 4:1 (NLT) regarding the discerning of false prophets – *"For there are many false prophets in the world."*
- The Apostle Peter wrote about the danger of false teachers – *"But there were also false prophets in Israel, just as there will be false teachers among you" - 2 Peter 2:1 (NLT).*
- Titus wrote about the multitude of rebellious people – *"For there are many rebellious people who engage in useless talk and deceive others" - Titus 1:10 (NLT).*
- Scripture was written in 2 John to make us aware of the antichrist deceiver – *"For many deceivers have gone out into the world who do not confess Jesus Christ as coming in the flesh. This is a deceiver and an antichrist" - 2 John 7 (NKJV).*
- Jude also recorded words warning us of false teachers – *"They brag about themselves with empty, foolish boasting. With an appeal to twisted sexual desires, they lure back into sin those who have barely escaped from a lifestyle of deception. They promise freedom, but they themselves are slaves of sin and corruption" Jude 3 (NLT).*
- Jude recorded Scriptures about scoffers who would arise in the last days – *"But you, my dear friends, must remember what the apostles of*

our Lord Jesus Christ predicted. They told you that in the last times there would be scoffers whose purpose in life is to satisfy their ungodly desires. These people are the ones who are creating divisions among you. They follow their natural instincts because they do not have God's Spirit in them" - Jude 17-19 (NLT).

- Perhaps the Apostle Peter gave the best description of false teaching. These individuals demonstrate the character of the tares; sons of the wicked one. Peter stated the following:

"These false teachers are like unthinking animals, creatures of instinct, born to be caught and destroyed. They scoff at things they do not understand, and like animals, they will be destroyed. Their destruction is their reward for the harm they have done. They love to indulge in evil pleasures in broad daylight. They are a disgrace and a stain among you. They delight in deception even as they eat with you in your fellowship meals. They commit adultery with their eyes, and their desire for sin is never satisfied. They lure unstable people into sin, and they are well trained in greed. They live under God's curse. They have wandered off the right road and followed the footsteps of Balaam son of Boer, who loved to earn money by doing wrong. But Balaam was stopped from his mad course when his donkey rebuked him with a human voice.

These people are as useless as dried-up springs or as mist blown away by the wind. They are doomed to blackest darkness. For you are slaves to whatever controls you. And when people escape from the wickedness of the world by knowing our Lord and Savior Jesus Christ and then get tangled up and enslaved by sin again, they are worse off than before. It would be better if they had never known the way to righteousness than to know it and then reject the command they were given to live a holy life" 2 Peter 2:12-21(NLT).

Please remember what Peter stated above, "You are a slave to whatever controls you!" If you remain in a situation of false teaching and obey the words of the church leader, you become a slave to his/her words. The

Apostle Paul recorded, "Do you not know that to whom you present yourselves slaves to obey, you are that one's slaves whom you obey, whether of sin leading to death, or of obedience leading to righteousness" Romans 6:16 (NKJV)? It then becomes a situation of the blind leading the blind! "When He [Jesus] had called the multitude to *Himself*, He said to them, "Hear and understand: Not what goes into the mouth defiles a man; but what comes out of the mouth, this defiles a man." Then His disciples came and said to Him, "Do You know that the Pharisees were offended when they heard this saying?" But He answered and said, "Every plant which My heavenly Father has not planted will be uprooted. Let them alone. They are blind leaders of the blind. And if the blind leads the blind, both will fall into a ditch." Matthew 15:10-14 (NKJV).

How to Take God's Kingdom by Force!

As shown above, the pathway to God's Kingdom has many obstacles. Remember Jesus' words, "But the gateway to life is very narrow and the road is difficult, and only a few ever find it" Matthew 7:14 (NLT). The road to life in God's Kingdom is difficult because of the obstacles. Nevertheless, Jesus also states, "And from the days of John the Baptist until now the kingdom of heaven suffers violence, and the violent take it by force" Matthew 11:12 (NKJV). Not only must one be faithful and obedient to Jesus Christ and the Word of the Kingdom, but they must also press their way into the Kingdom!

The violence that the Kingdom of God suffers is in reference to the antagonism of the enemies of the kingdom such as Satan and his angels of righteousness that have infiltrated churches worldwide. Entering the Kingdom violently illustrates those who make an effort to enter the kingdom in spite of violent opposition. I hate to say it but Satan has been on his job since the world was formed. "The thief does not come except to steal, and to kill, and to destroy" John 10:10 (NKJV). Therefore, he and his angels constantly throw-up road blocks in front of faithful believers in order to discourage them from advancing into God's Kingdom. He has to work extremely hard against believers who are determined and who will not give up! The obstacles are many. Satan's angels are the tares known as the sons of the wicked one; he simply keeps things before them that stimulate the lust and desires of their flesh. He has further deceived his angels of righteousness, false teachers and ministers, to preach a gospel that stimulates believers to seek the things of this world instead of living a sacrificial life, holy and acceptable to God.

I realize that most Christians believe they are rightly serving the Lord, being obedient and doing the things He desire! Furthermore, the things I write, even if they sound good, may not have any impact whatsoever on your beliefs. Just remember, there has been a pattern of deception in God's people since the beginning of time. Those deceived in the past thought they were serving God correctly and following His commandments, His desires and His will on earth. Initially, there was Adam and Eve, and then it was God's chosen people, the Jews. Today it is millions of Christians who involve themselves in some level of Christianity, but not the truth of God's Word! God's Word clearly revealed Satan's deception and how it would influence the heart and mind of God's people, both congregants and leaders. There is a pattern of God's leaders being widely deceived, especially in the Jewish nation. Many of today's church leaders are just replicas of the scribes, Pharisees and Sadducees.

Deception occurs when God's truth and the fullness of His counsel are not preached and taught to His people. A clear example of this is the failure of Jesus' servants (the fivefold ministry) to do as He did and preach the _only_ healing message He taught to His followers: The Kingdom of God and its mysteries!

The Gospel and the Great Commission!
"Then Jesus went about all the cities and villages, teaching in their synagogues, preaching the gospel of the kingdom, and healing every sickness and every disease among the people" Matthew 9:35 (NKJV).

"Later He appeared to the eleven as they sat at the table; and He [Jesus] rebuked their unbelief and hardness of heart, because they did not believe those who had seen Him after He had risen. And He said to them, "Go into all the world and preach the gospel [Gospel of the Kingdom] to every creature. He

who believes and is baptized will be saved; but he who does not believe will be condemned" "Mark 16:14-16 (NKJV).

Today's ministers often label their messages as the Kingdom of God, but few give clarity and revelation of the mysteries and secrets of the Kingdom. Jesus taught the message that healed every sickness and every disease among the people, both physical and spiritual healing. Make no mistake about it, He commissioned every servant thereafter to do the same. Unfortunately, the majority of today's Christians only hear a message of the *flesh*: How they can proper, what the Lord will do for them, how their ship and harvest is on the way and more. You know what I'm talking about! We must never forget that all creation was subject to vanity (Excessive pride in one's appearance or accomplishments; conceit. Something that is vain, futile, or worthless). *Only* the Gospel of the Kingdom message can and will deliver God's people from this bondage and make them worthy to become the children of God. "For the creature was made subject to vanity, not willingly, but by reason of him who hath subjected the same in hope, because the creature itself also shall be delivered from the bondage of corruption into the glorious liberty of the children of God" Romans 8:20-21 (KJV).

I have attempted, many times to reveal spiritual blindness to today's Christians so that they can understand why so many people are being deceived. However, it is almost impossible to do. Jesus was unable to convince the Jews of their blindness and likewise today, Christians do not understand nor discern spiritual blindness themselves!

"And in them the prophecy of Isaiah is fulfilled, which says: 'Hearing you will hear and shall not understand, and seeing you will see and not perceive; for the hearts of this people have grown dull. Their ears are hard of hearing, and their eyes they have closed, lest they should see with their eyes and hear with their ears, lest they should understand with their hearts and turn, so that I should heal them" Matthew 13:14-15 (NKJV).

Here is the problem: There are few Christians who desire, covet, hunger and/or crave after the revelation and hidden things of God's Word. If you seek truth, God will give it to you in response to your prayers. "Keep on asking, and you will receive what you ask for. Keep on seeking, and you will find. Keep on knocking, and the door will be opened to you. For everyone who asks, receives. Everyone who seeks, finds. And to everyone who knocks, the door will be opened" Matthew 7:7-8 (NLT). Believers, who with their mind and heart, press to know the truth will be given the truth! We already know to encourage faithful believers to continue in the faith, reminding them that we must suffer many hardships to enter the Kingdom of God. Those who are serious-minded, press their way into God's Kingdom. "The law and the prophets were until John. Since that time the kingdom of God has been preached, and everyone is pressing into it" Luke 16:16 (NKJV). Paul said that "He press toward the goal for the prize of the upward call of God in Christ Jesus" Philippians 3:14 (NKJV). And so do we; those who are determined to obtain life in the Kingdom of heaven. Paul further stated, "Not that I have already attained, or am already perfected; but I press on, that I may lay hold of that for which Christ Jesus has also laid hold of me. Brethren, I do not count myself to have apprehended; but one thing I do, forgetting those things which are behind and reaching forward to those things which are ahead, I press toward the goal for the prize of the upward call of God in Christ Jesus" Philippians 3:12-14 (NKJV).

Believers take the Kingdom by force under the leading and guidance of the Holy Spirit. It comes to you no other way! The pressing and the forcing come by the spiritual guiding and anointing of God's Spirit! It is the Spirit that gives us power to endure, overcome and press through the obstacles of this life and the wiles of Satan. In the parable of the ten virgins, only the five wise virgins that lived according to the Spirit were able to attend the wedding feast and then the door was shut. This is the formula for taking the Kingdom by force. As stated in Zechariah, "So he answered and said to me: "This is the word of the LORD to Zerubbabel: 'Not by might nor by power, but by My Spirit,' Says the LORD of hosts" Zechariah 4:6 (NKJV). We enter and/or inherit God's Kingdom by the power from on high! It is God's Spirit *in us* that allows us to press into the Kingdom. This occurs to those who become believers and are empowered by the Spirit of God. They are indwelled by Him and exercise His power for God's glory, not theirs!

A Final Word from the Author

There are many Christians in the body of Christ who do not understand why God's people must endure trials, tribulations, tests, chastisements, hardships, afflictions, and sufferings. Yet we know that Jesus Christ stated, "But he who endures to the end shall be saved" Matthew 24:13 (NKJV). It is when we endure and overcome all of the trials and tribulations of this life, which includes the battles we face against the god of this world, that we become God's children. It is under the anointing power of God's Spirit that true life comes available to us! In this, we prove our love, faith and obedience to Jesus Christ. "And they overcame him by the _blood of the Lamb_ and by the word of their _testimony_, and they _did not love_ their lives to the death" Revelation 12:11 (NKJV). Our _testimony_ is the account of how the power of God delivered us from the bondage of corruption into the glorious liberty of a child of God. The simplicity of the Gospel is love, thrust and obedience to Jesus Christ. There are many voices in the land teaching many facets of the Gospel and God's promises, but when judgment day comes, we will be _evaluated_ by the love, thrust and obedience we have given to Jesus Christ, our Lord and Savior! *Are you ready?*

    John Elliott Williams

Other Christian Books written by John Elliott Williams

Only A Few!
Those who do not defile God's Temple!
Jesus said, "Difficult is the way which leads to life and there are few who find it" (Matthew 7:14)
John Elliott Williams

Made in the USA
Las Vegas, NV
11 July 2024

92171908R00095